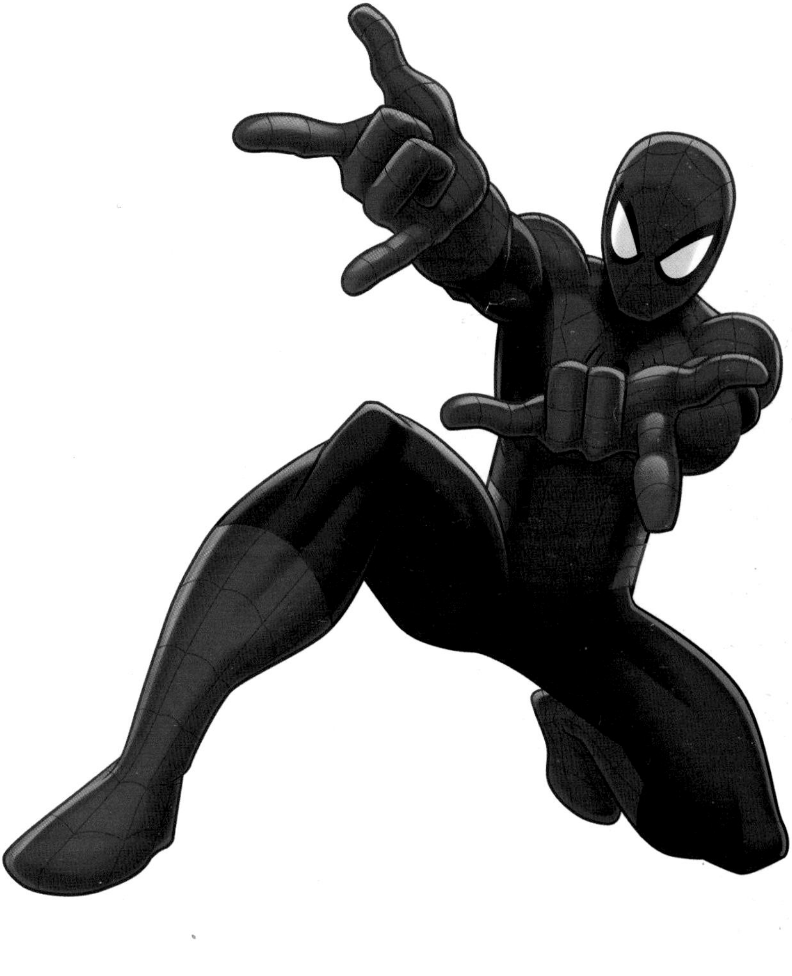

17

Based on **"Field Trip"**

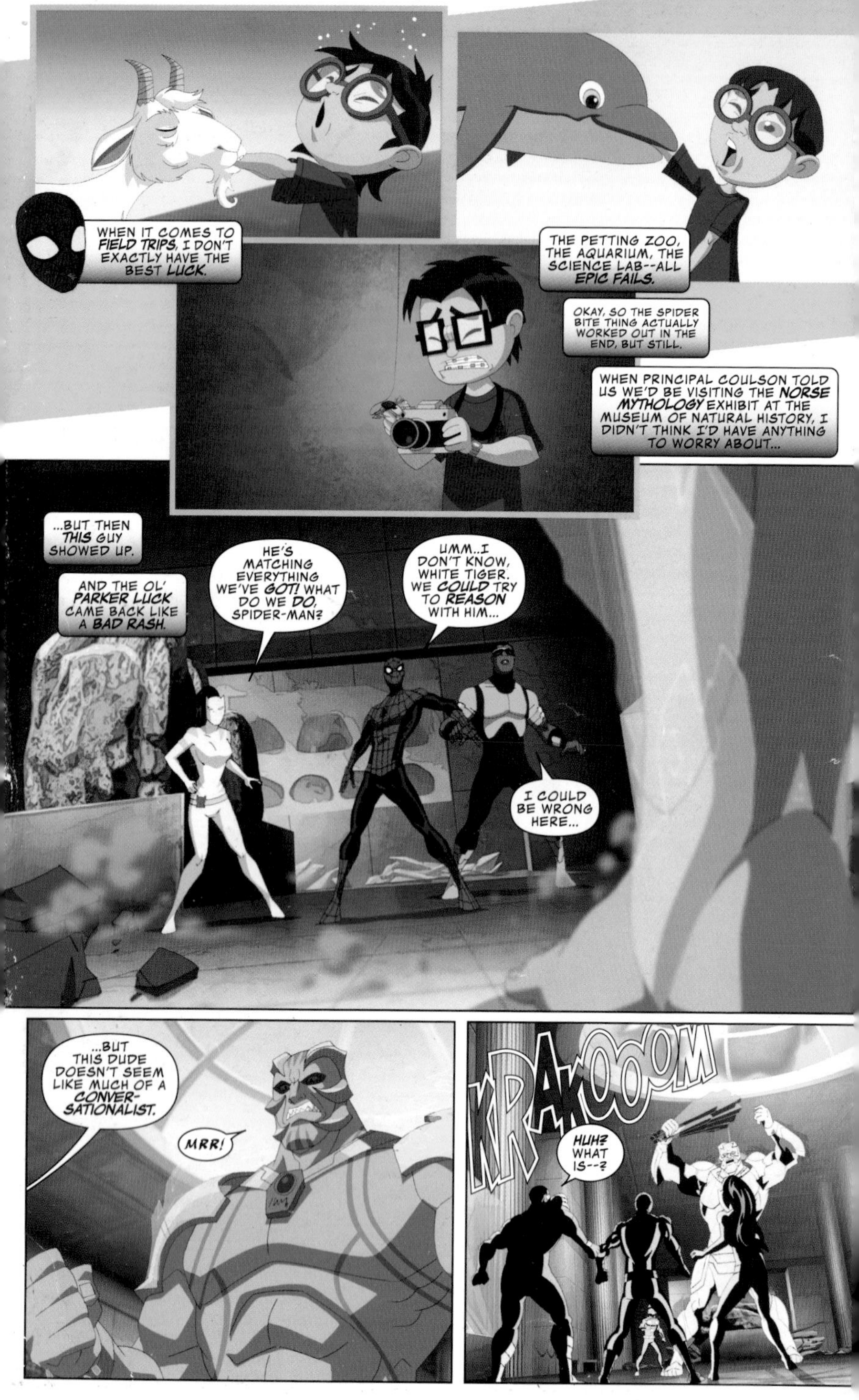
WHEN IT COMES TO FIELD TRIPS, I DON'T EXACTLY HAVE THE BEST LUCK.
THE PETTING ZOO, THE AQUARIUM, THE SCIENCE LAB--ALL EPIC FAILS.
OKAY, SO THE SPIDER BITE THING ACTUALLY WORKED OUT IN THE END, BUT STILL.
WHEN PRINCIPAL COULSON TOLD US WE'D BE VISITING THE NORSE MYTHOLOGY EXHIBIT AT THE MUSEUM OF NATURAL HISTORY, I DIDN'T THINK I'D HAVE ANYTHING TO WORRY ABOUT...
...BUT THEN THIS GUY SHOWED UP.
AND THE OL' PARKER LUCK CAME BACK LIKE A BAD RASH.
HE'S MATCHING EVERYTHING WE'VE GOT! WHAT DO WE DO, SPIDER-MAN?
UMM..I DON'T KNOW, WHITE TIGER. WE COULD TRY TO REASON WITH HIM...
I COULD BE WRONG HERE...
...BUT THIS DUDE DOESN'T SEEM LIKE MUCH OF A CONVER-SATIONALIST.
MRR!
KRAKOOOM
HUH? WHAT IS--?

MARVEL UNIVERSE ULTIMATE SPIDER-MAN VOL. 5. Contains material originally published in magazine form as MARVEL UNIVERSE ULTIMATE SPIDER-MAN #17-20. First printing 2014. ISBN# 978-0-7851-8814-8. Published by MARVEL WORLDWIDE, INC., a subsidiary of MARVEL ENTERTAINMENT, LLC. OFFICE OF PUBLICATION: 135 West 50th Street, New York, NY 10020. Copyright © 2013 and 2014 Marvel Characters, Inc. All characters featured in this issue and the distinctive names and likenesses thereof, and all related indicia are trademarks of Marvel Characters, Inc. No similarity between any of the names, characters, persons, and/or institutions in this magazine with those of any living or dead person or institution is intended, and any such similarity which may exist is purely coincidental. **Printed in the U.S.A.** ALAN FINE, EVP - Office of the President, Marvel Worldwide, Inc. and EVP & CMO Marvel Characters B.V.; DAN BUCKLEY, Publisher & President - Print, Animation & Digital Divisions; JOE QUESADA, Chief Creative Officer; TOM BREVOORT, SVP of Publishing; DAVID BOGART, SVP of Operations & Procurement, Publishing; C.B. CEBULSKI, SVP of Creator & Content Development; DAVID GABRIEL, SVP of Print & Digital Publishing Sales; JIM O'KEEFE, VP of Operations & Logistics; DAN CARR, Exec...SALES, Publishing Operations Manager; STAN LE...n, please contact Niza Disla, Director of Marvel..B. **Manufactured between 11/29/2013 and 1/.....**

10 9 8 7 6 5 4 3 2 1

C333516320

MARVEL ULTIMATE SPIDER-MAN

BASED ON THE TV SERIES BY

MAN OF ACTION, EUGENE SON, BRIAN MICHAEL BENDIS & JACOB SEMAHN

ADAPTED BY

JOE CARAMAGNA

EDITOR

SEBASTIAN GIRNER

CONSULTING EDITOR

JON MOISAN

SENIOR EDITOR

MARK PANICCIA

Collection Editor: **Cory Levine**
Assistant Editors: **Alex Starbuck & Nelson Ribeiro**
Editors, Special Projects: **Jennifer Grünwald & Mark D. Beazley**
Senior Editor, Special Projects: **Jeff Youngquist**
SVP of Print & Digital Publishing Sales: **David Gabriel**
Head of Marvel Television: **Jeph Loeb**

Editor In Chief: **Axel Alonso**
Chief Creative Officer: **Joe Quesada**
Publisher: **Dan Buckley**
Executive Producer: **Alan Fine**

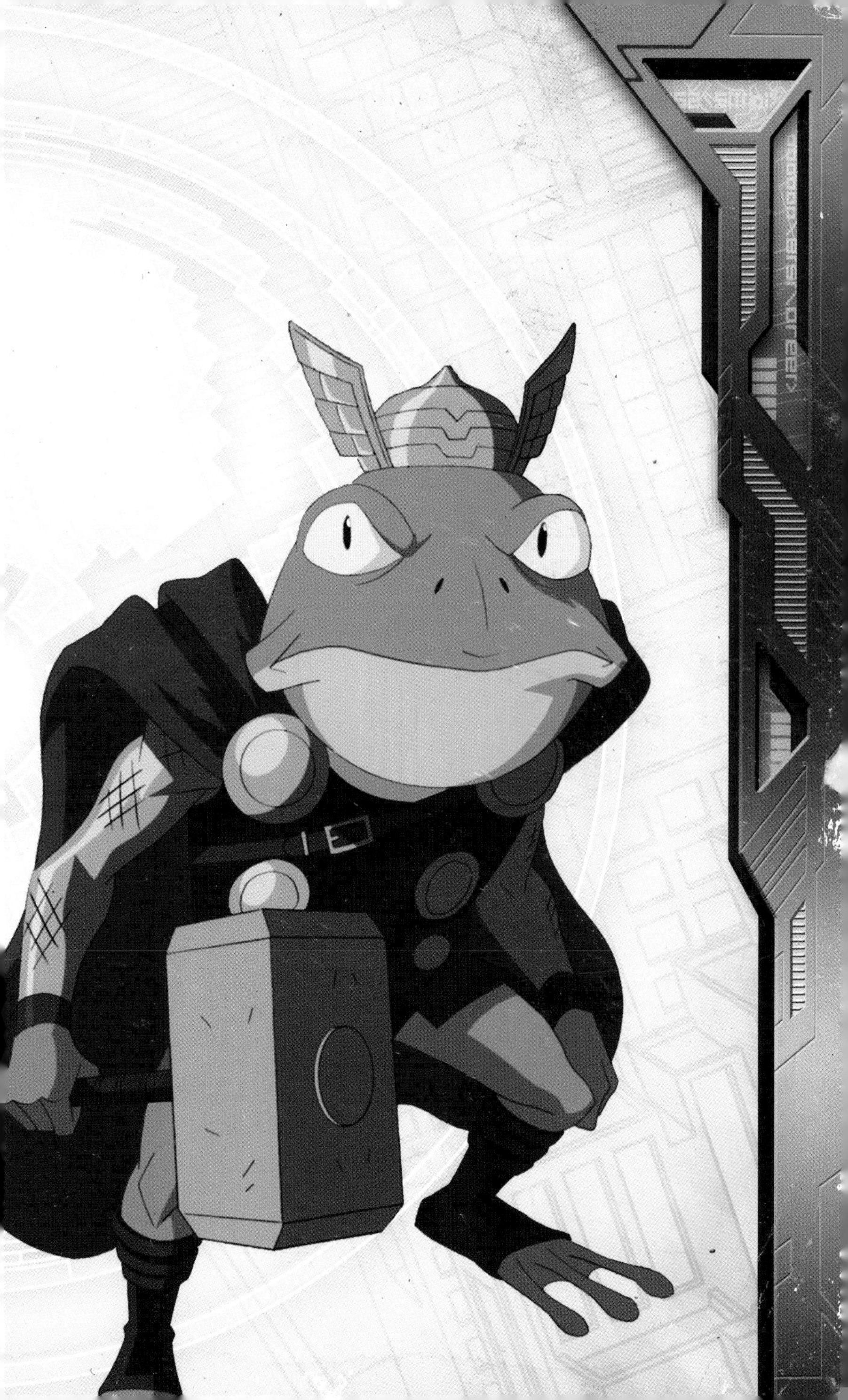

While attending a demonstration in radiology, high school student Peter Parker was bitten by a spider that had accidentally been exposed to radioactive rays. Through a miracle of science, Peter soon found that he had gained the spider's powers...and had, in effect, become a human spider! From that day on, he has endeavored to become the...

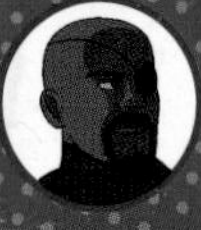
Nick Fury

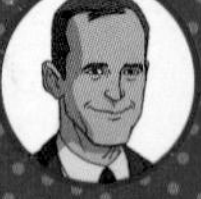
Principal Coulson

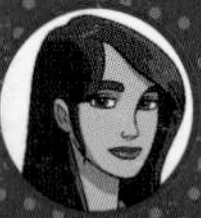
Mary Jane Watson

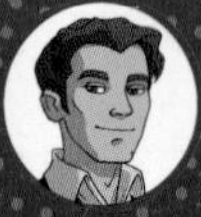
Harry Osborn

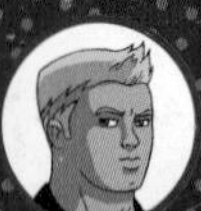
Flash Thompson

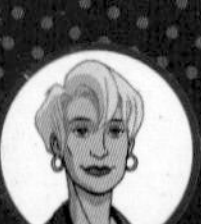
Aunt May

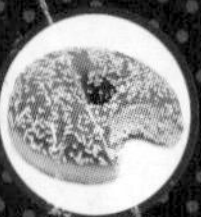
A Donut (yum!)

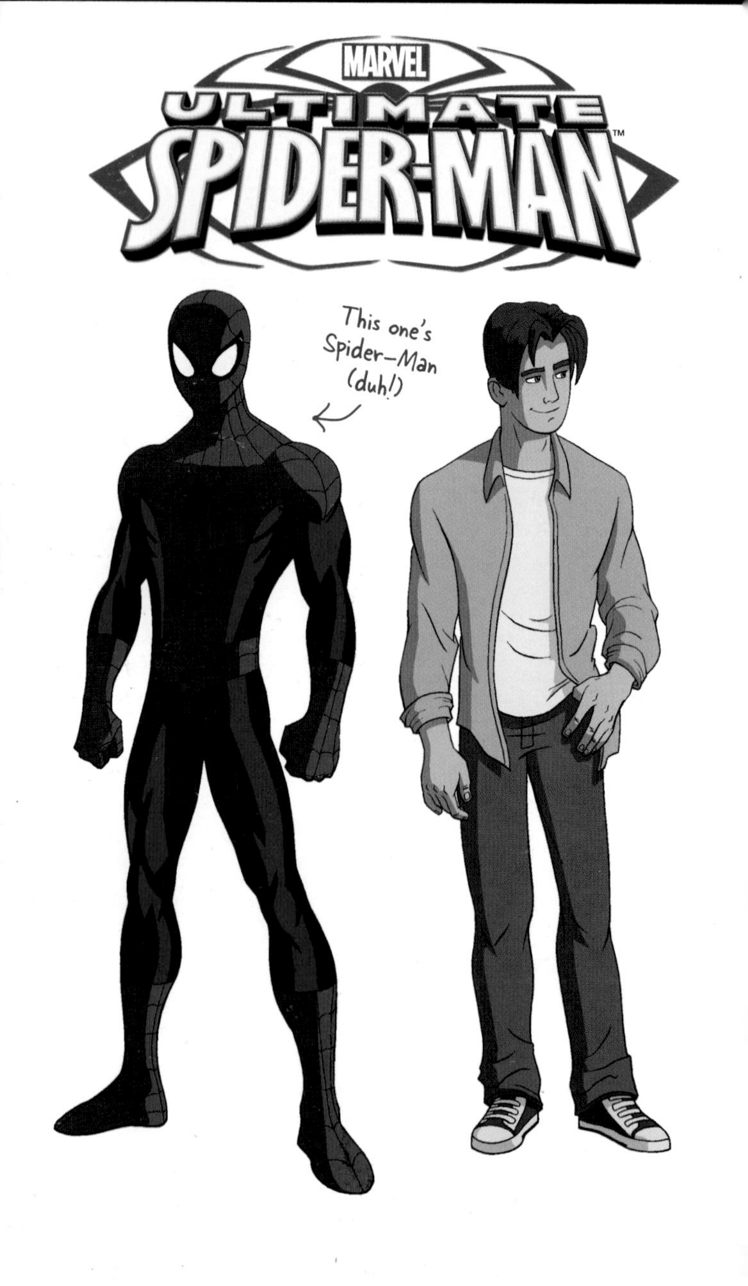
MARVEL
ULTIMATE SPIDER-MAN™
This one's Spider-Man (duh!)

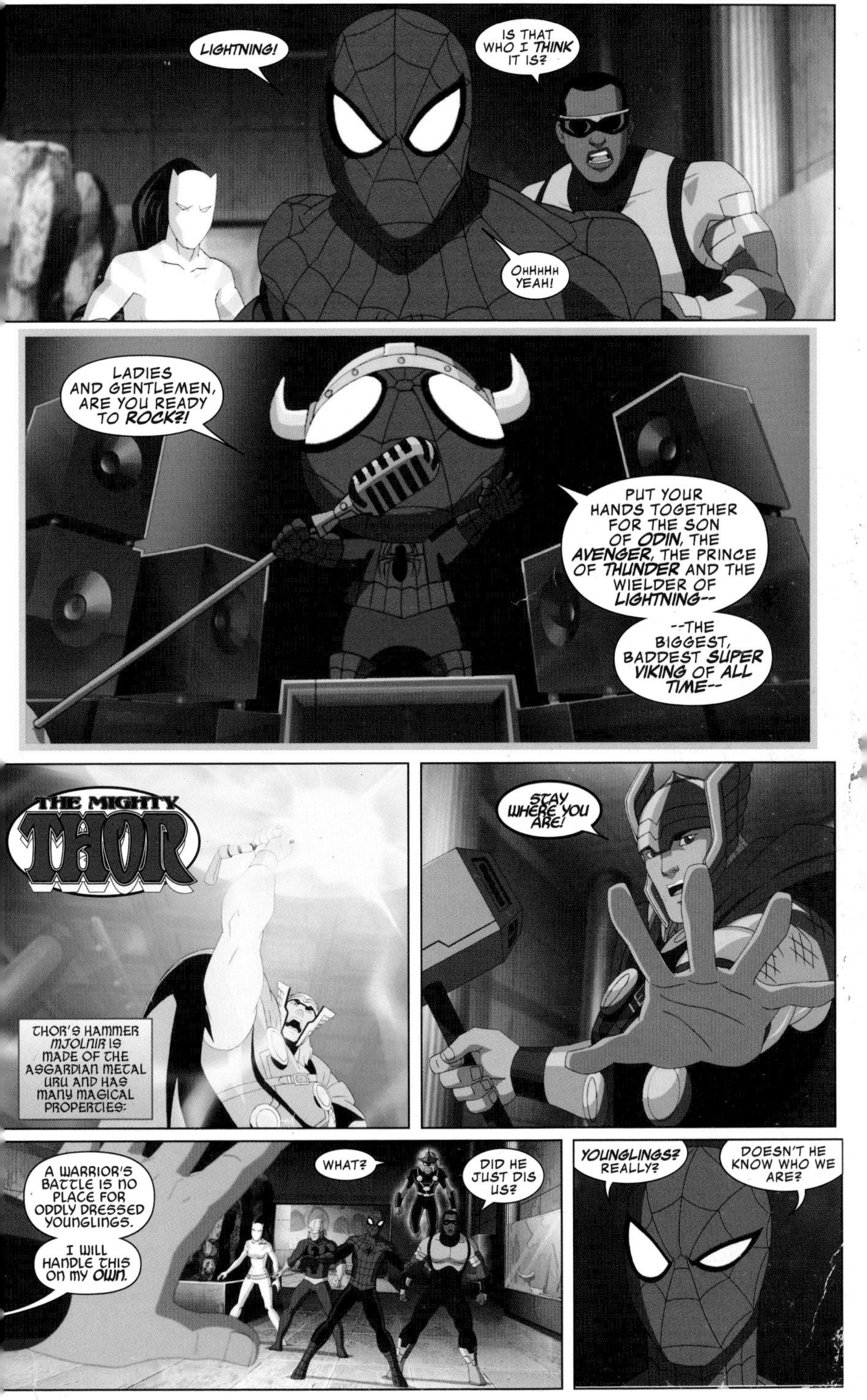
LIGHTNING!
IS THAT WHO I THINK IT IS?
OHHHHH YEAH!
LADIES AND GENTLEMEN, ARE YOU READY TO ROCK?!
PUT YOUR HANDS TOGETHER FOR THE SON OF ODIN, THE AVENGER, THE PRINCE OF THUNDER AND THE WIELDER OF LIGHTNING--
--THE BIGGEST, BADDEST SUPER VIKING OF ALL TIME--
THE MIGHTY THOR
THOR'S HAMMER MJOLNIR IS MADE OF THE ASGARDIAN METAL URU AND HAS MANY MAGICAL PROPERTIES.
STAY WHERE YOU ARE!
A WARRIOR'S BATTLE IS NO PLACE FOR ODDLY DRESSED YOUNGLINGS.
I WILL HANDLE THIS ON MY OWN.
WHAT?
DID HE JUST DIS US?
YOUNGLINGS? REALLY?
DOESN'T HE KNOW WHO WE ARE?

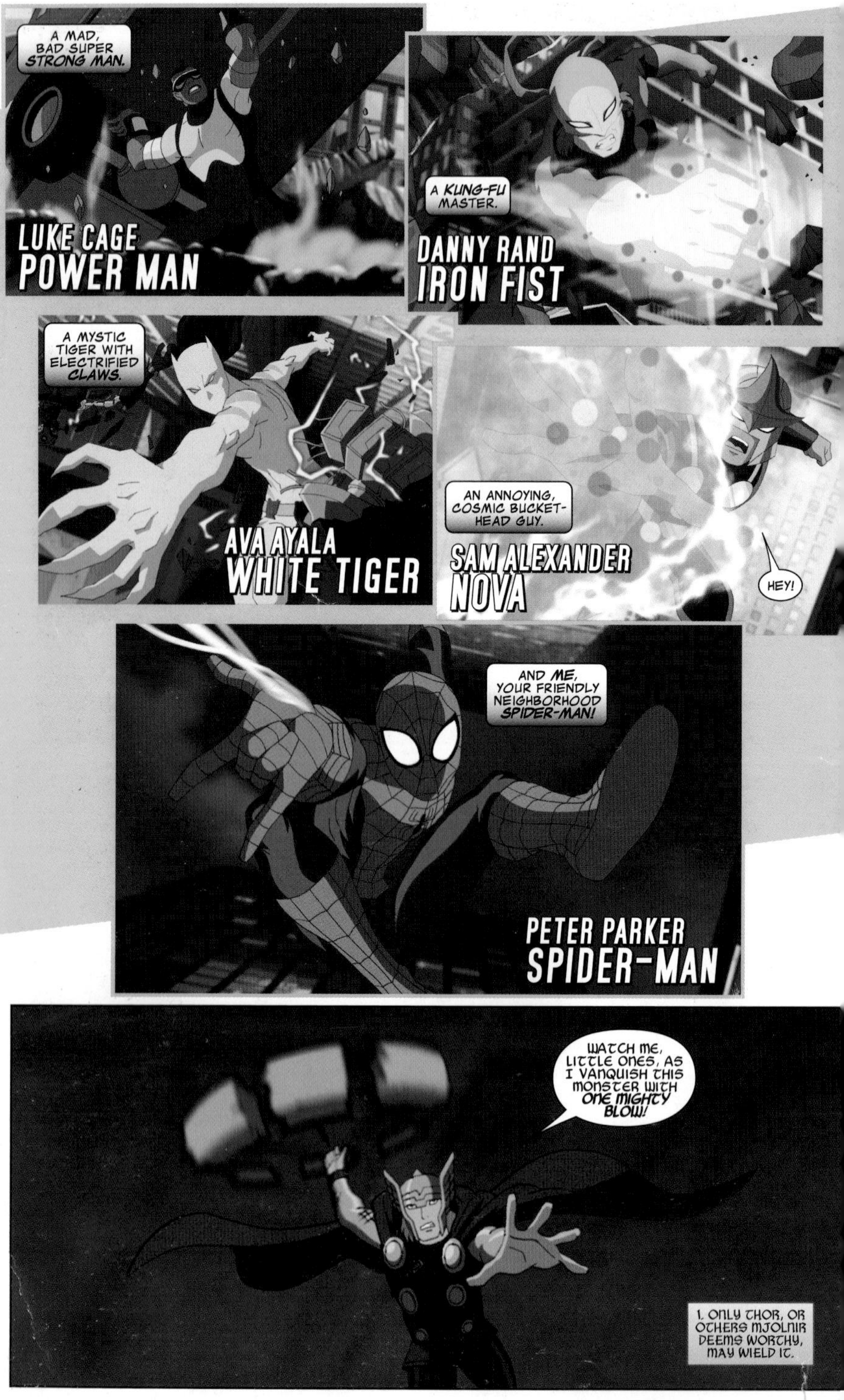
A MAD, BAD SUPER STRONG MAN.
LUKE CAGE
POWER MAN
A KUNG-FU MASTER.
DANNY RAND
IRON FIST
A MYSTIC TIGER WITH ELECTRIFIED CLAWS.
AVA AYALA
WHITE TIGER
AN ANNOYING, COSMIC BUCKET-HEAD GUY.
SAM ALEXANDER
NOVA
HEY!
AND ME, YOUR FRIENDLY NEIGHBORHOOD SPIDER-MAN!
PETER PARKER
SPIDER-MAN
WATCH ME, LITTLE ONES, AS I VANQUISH THIS MONSTER WITH ONE MIGHTY BLOW!
1. ONLY THOR, OR OTHERS MJOLNIR DEEMS WORTHY, MAY WIELD IT.

BRAKKOOM

MY WORK HERE IS DONE.

FWAP

2. WHEN THROWN, NO OBSTACLE CAN KEEP MJOLNIR FROM RETURNING TO THOR'S HAND.

HM. THAT IS RATHER UNUSUAL *NECKWEAR* FOR A *FROST GIANT*.

LET'S FACE IT--THOR'S JUST A BIG, ARROGANT *JERK*. AND HE BUTTED IN ON *OUR* FIGHT.

WHAT ARE WE GOING TO DO ABOUT THIS, FEARLESS LEADER?

ME? WHAT CAN *I* DO ABOUT HIM? HE'S AN *AVENGER!* THAT'S WAY ABOVE MY--

SPIDER-SENSE!

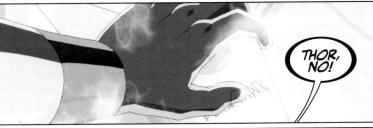

THOR, NO!

DON'T TOUCH THAAAAAAAAHHHH!

FWASH!

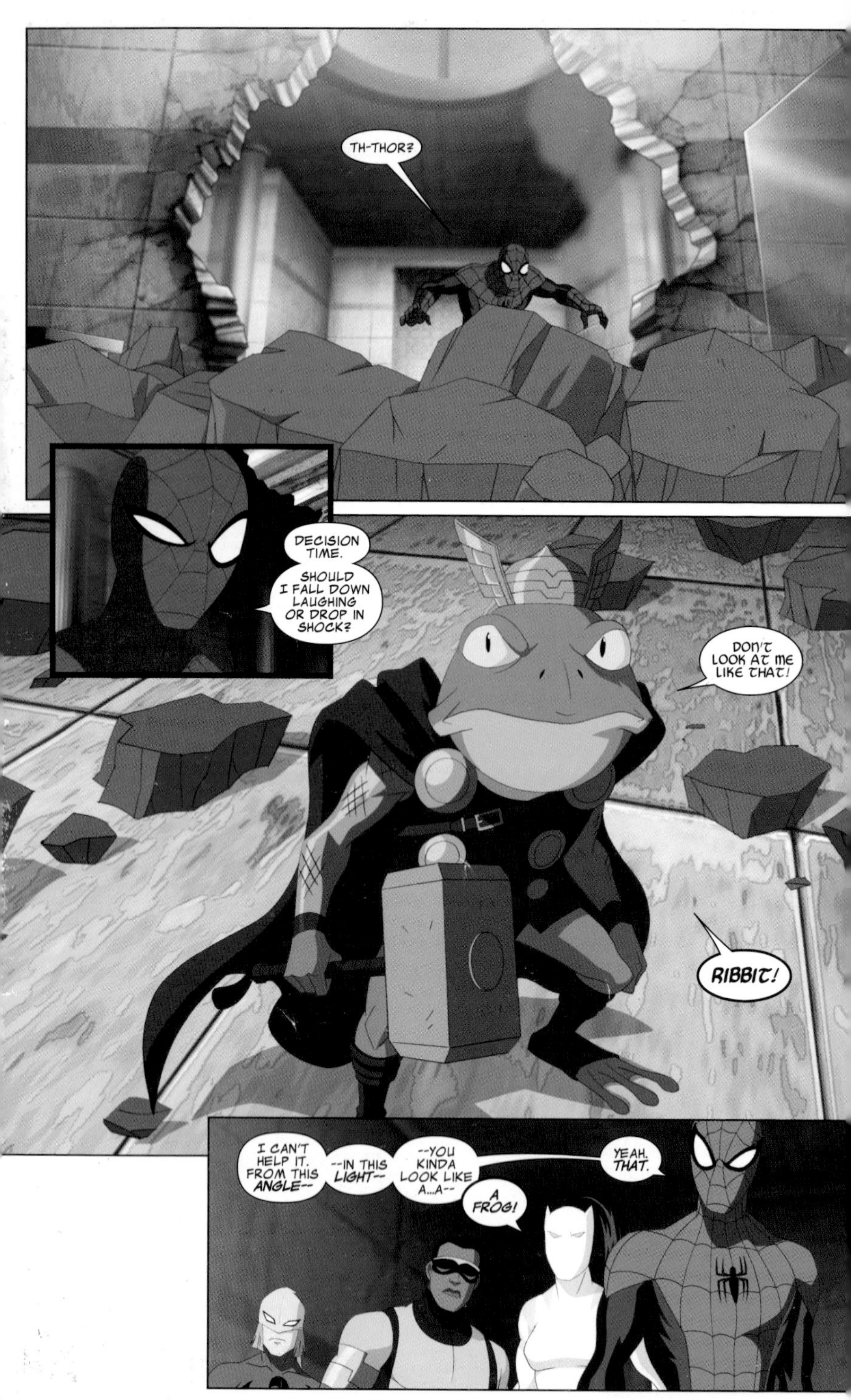
TH-THOR?
DECISION TIME.
SHOULD I FALL DOWN LAUGHING OR DROP IN SHOCK?
DON'T LOOK AT ME LIKE THAT!
RIBBIT!
I CAN'T HELP IT. FROM THIS ANGLE--
--IN THIS LIGHT--
--YOU KINDA LOOK LIKE A...A--
A FROG!
YEAH. THAT.

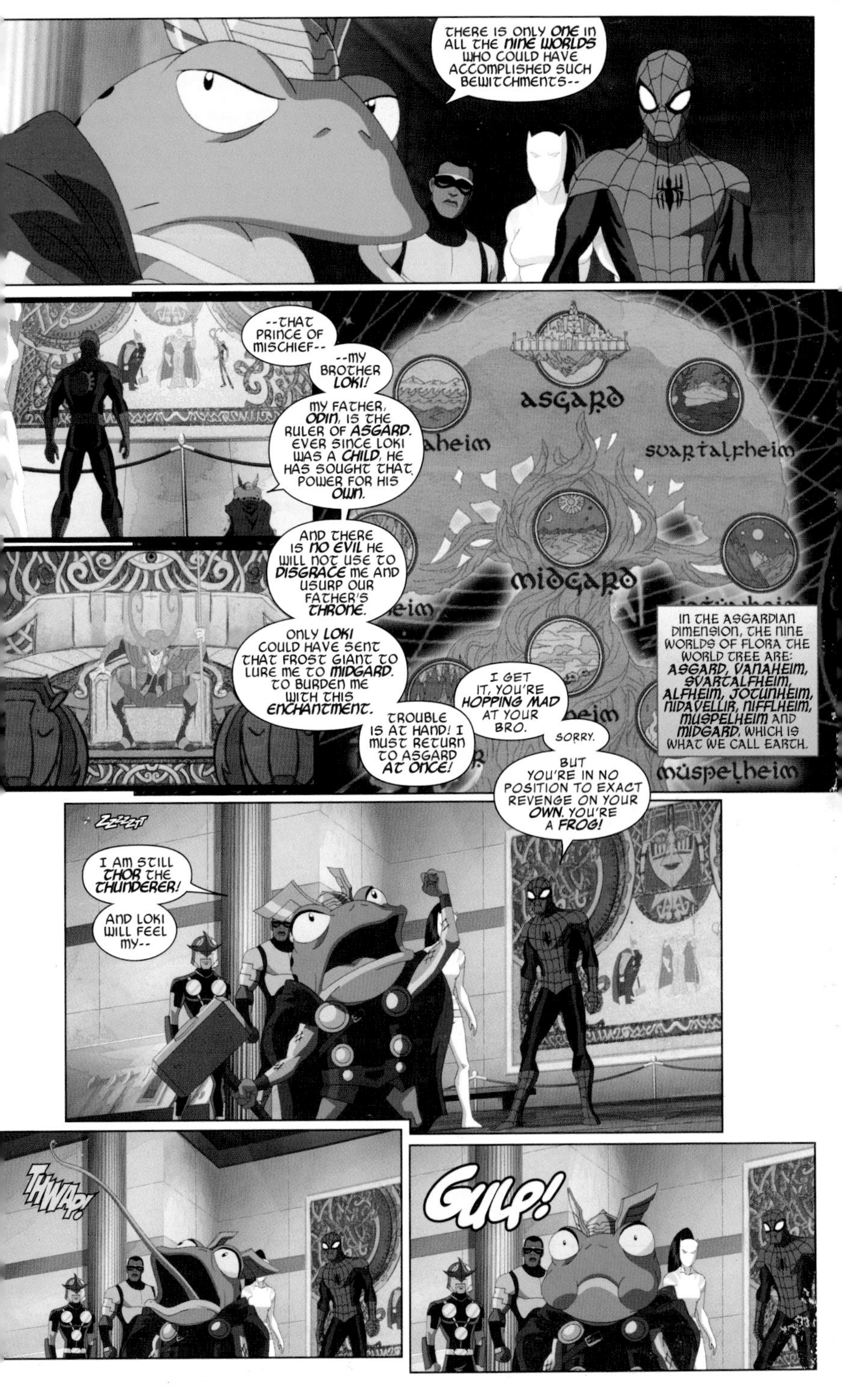
THERE IS ONLY ONE IN ALL THE NINE WORLDS WHO COULD HAVE ACCOMPLISHED SUCH BEWITCHMENTS--
--THAT PRINCE OF MISCHIEF--
--MY BROTHER LOKI!
MY FATHER, ODIN, IS THE RULER OF ASGARD. EVER SINCE LOKI WAS A CHILD, HE HAS SOUGHT THAT POWER FOR HIS OWN.
AND THERE IS NO EVIL HE WILL NOT USE TO DISGRACE ME AND USURP OUR FATHER'S THRONE.
ONLY LOKI COULD HAVE SENT THAT FROST GIANT TO LURE ME TO MIDGARD. TO BURDEN ME WITH THIS ENCHANTMENT.
ASGARD
SVARTALFHEIM
MIDGARD
MUSPELHEIM
IN THE ASGARDIAN DIMENSION, THE NINE WORLDS OF FLORA THE WORLD TREE ARE: ASGARD, VANAHEIM, SVARTALFHEIM, ALFHEIM, JOTUNHEIM, NIDAVELLIR, NIFFLHEIM, MUSPELHEIM AND MIDGARD, WHICH IS WHAT WE CALL EARTH.
I GET IT, YOU'RE HOPPING MAD AT YOUR BRO.
TROUBLE IS AT HAND! I MUST RETURN TO ASGARD AT ONCE!
SORRY.
BUT YOU'RE IN NO POSITION TO EXACT REVENGE ON YOUR OWN. YOU'RE A FROG!
ZZZZZT
I AM STILL THOR THE THUNDERER!
AND LOKI WILL FEEL MY--
THWAP!
GULP!

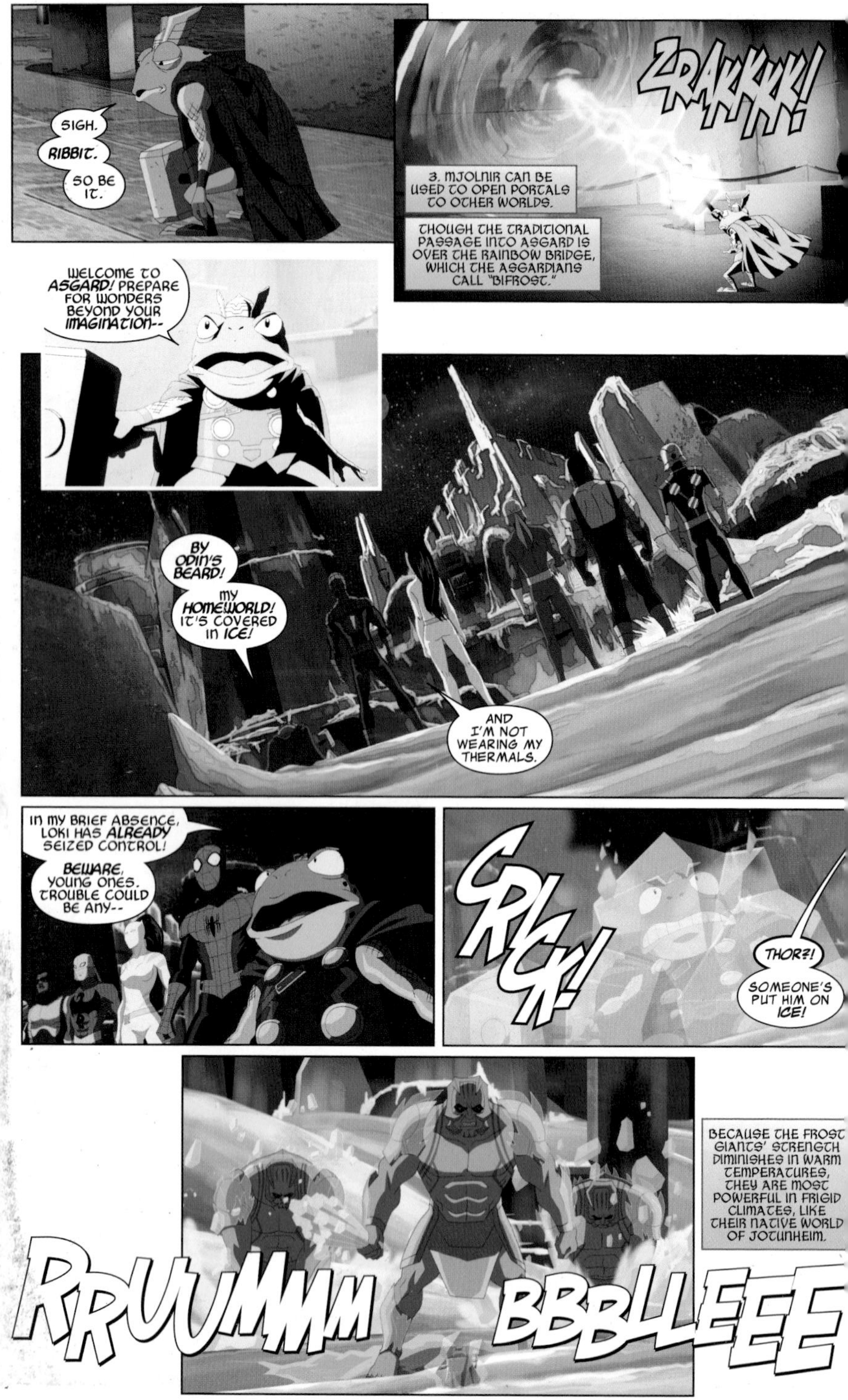

SIGH.
RIBBIT.
SO BE IT.
ZRAKKK!
3. MJOLNIR CAN BE USED TO OPEN PORTALS TO OTHER WORLDS.
THOUGH THE TRADITIONAL PASSAGE INTO ASGARD IS OVER THE RAINBOW BRIDGE, WHICH THE ASGARDIANS CALL "BIFROST."
WELCOME TO ASGARD! PREPARE FOR WONDERS BEYOND YOUR IMAGINATION--
BY ODIN'S BEARD!
MY HOMEWORLD! IT'S COVERED IN ICE!
AND I'M NOT WEARING MY THERMALS.
IN MY BRIEF ABSENCE, LOKI HAS ALREADY SEIZED CONTROL!
BEWARE, YOUNG ONES. TROUBLE COULD BE ANY--
CRACK!
THOR?!
SOMEONE'S PUT HIM ON ICE!
BECAUSE THE FROST GIANTS' STRENGTH DIMINISHES IN WARM TEMPERATURES, THEY ARE MOST POWERFUL IN FRIGID CLIMATES, LIKE THEIR NATIVE WORLD OF JOTUNHEIM.
RRUUMMMM BBBLLEEE

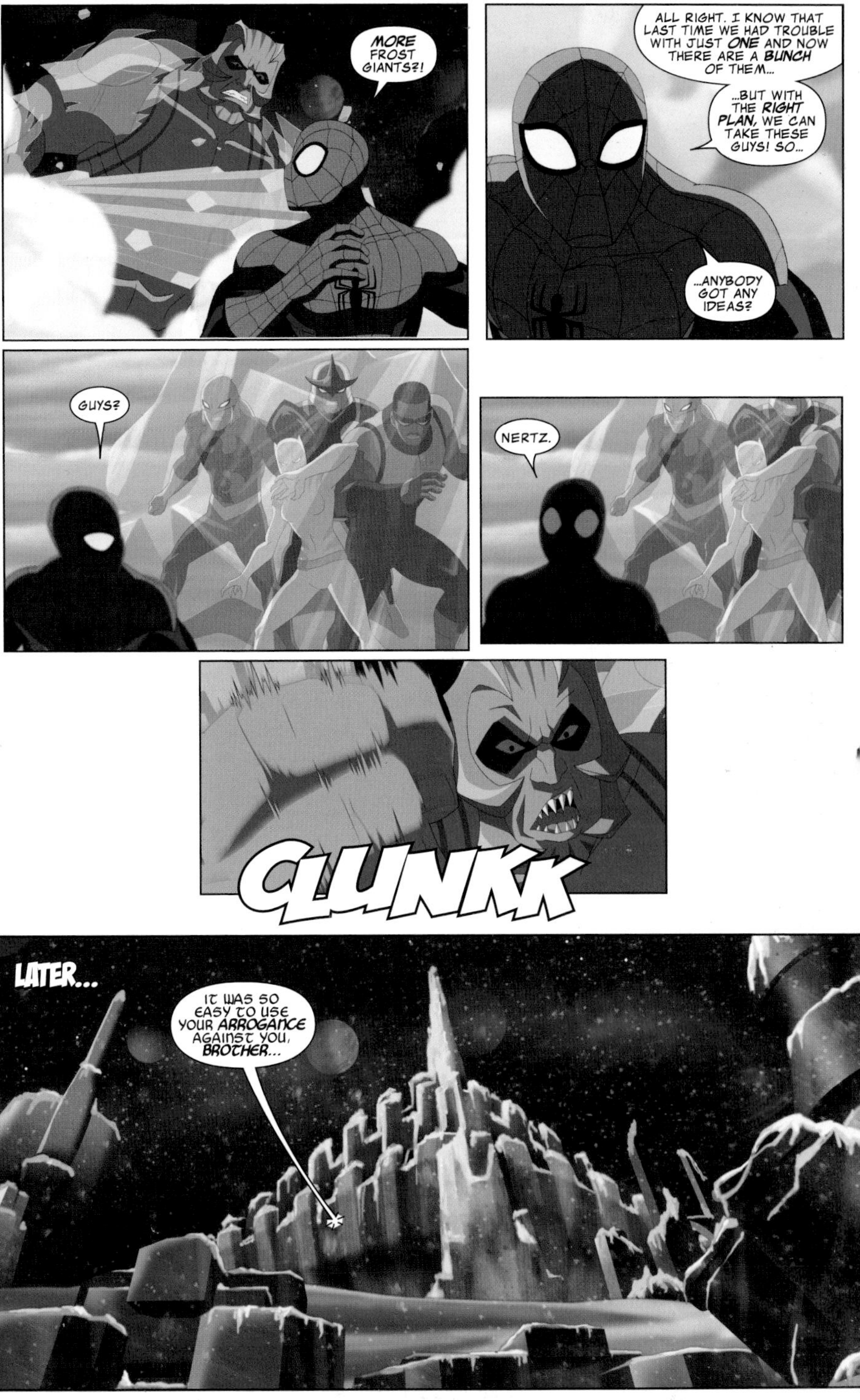
MORE FROST GIANTS?!
ALL RIGHT. I KNOW THAT LAST TIME WE HAD TROUBLE WITH JUST ONE AND NOW THERE ARE A BUNCH OF THEM...
...BUT WITH THE RIGHT PLAN, WE CAN TAKE THESE GUYS! SO...
...ANYBODY GOT ANY IDEAS?
GUYS?
NERTZ.
CLUNKK
LATER...
IT WAS SO EASY TO USE YOUR ARROGANCE AGAINST YOU, BROTHER...

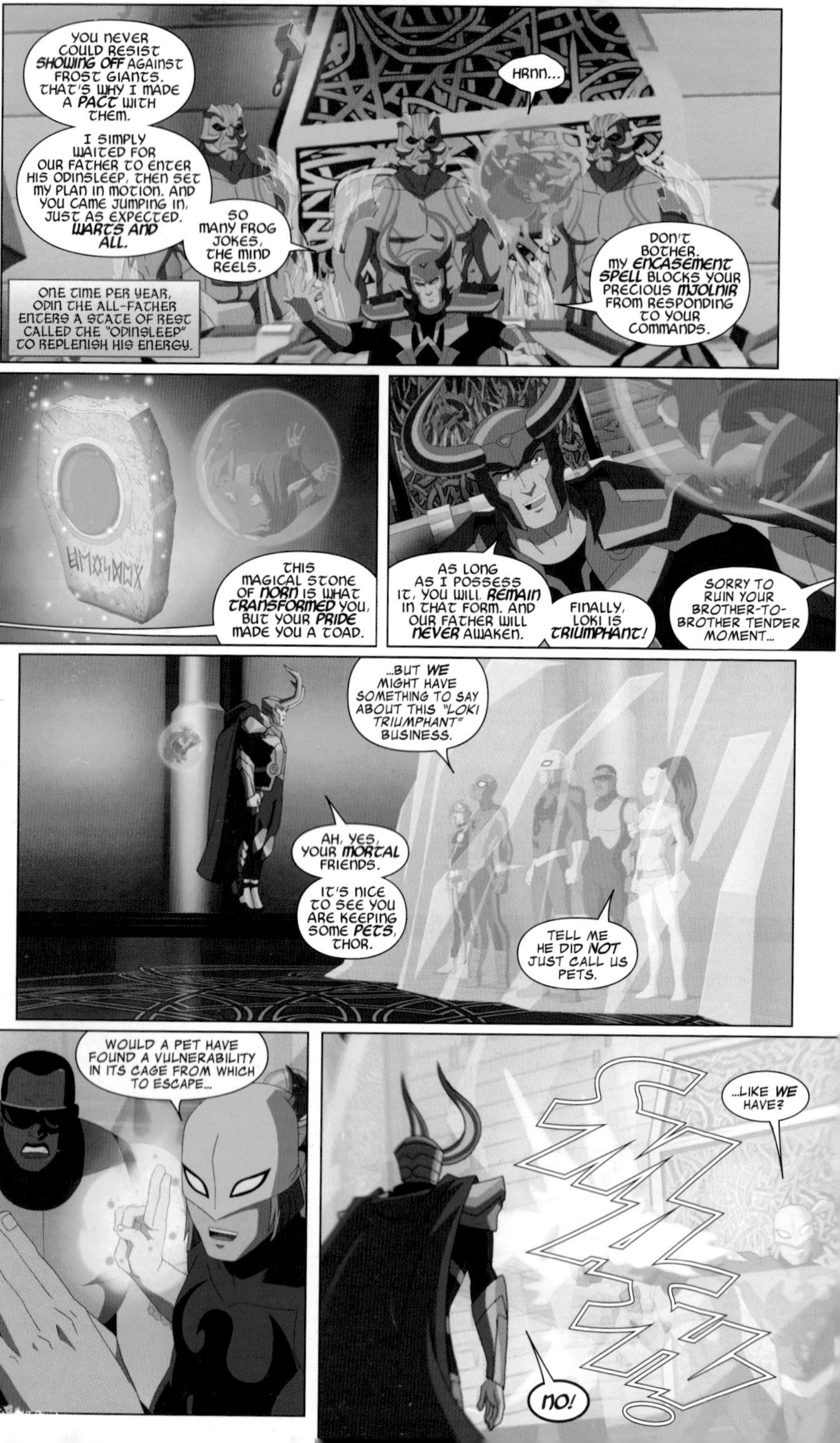
YOU NEVER COULD RESIST SHOWING OFF AGAINST FROST GIANTS. THAT'S WHY I MADE A PACT WITH THEM.
I SIMPLY WAITED FOR OUR FATHER TO ENTER HIS ODINSLEEP, THEN SET MY PLAN IN MOTION. AND YOU CAME JUMPING IN, JUST AS EXPECTED. WARTS AND ALL.
HRNN...
SO MANY FROG JOKES, THE MIND REELS.
ONE TIME PER YEAR, ODIN THE ALL-FATHER ENTERS A STATE OF REST CALLED THE "ODINSLEEP" TO REPLENISH HIS ENERGY.
DON'T BOTHER. MY ENCASEMENT SPELL BLOCKS YOUR PRECIOUS MJOLNIR FROM RESPONDING TO YOUR COMMANDS.
THIS MAGICAL STONE OF NORN IS WHAT TRANSFORMED YOU, BUT YOUR PRIDE MADE YOU A TOAD.
AS LONG AS I POSSESS IT, YOU WILL REMAIN IN THAT FORM. AND OUR FATHER WILL NEVER AWAKEN.
FINALLY, LOKI IS TRIUMPHANT!
SORRY TO RUIN YOUR BROTHER-TO-BROTHER TENDER MOMENT...
...BUT WE MIGHT HAVE SOMETHING TO SAY ABOUT THIS "LOKI TRIUMPHANT" BUSINESS.
AH, YES, YOUR MORTAL FRIENDS.
IT'S NICE TO SEE YOU ARE KEEPING SOME PETS, THOR.
TELL ME HE DID NOT JUST CALL US PETS.
WOULD A PET HAVE FOUND A VULNERABILITY IN ITS CAGE FROM WHICH TO ESCAPE...
...LIKE WE HAVE?
NO!

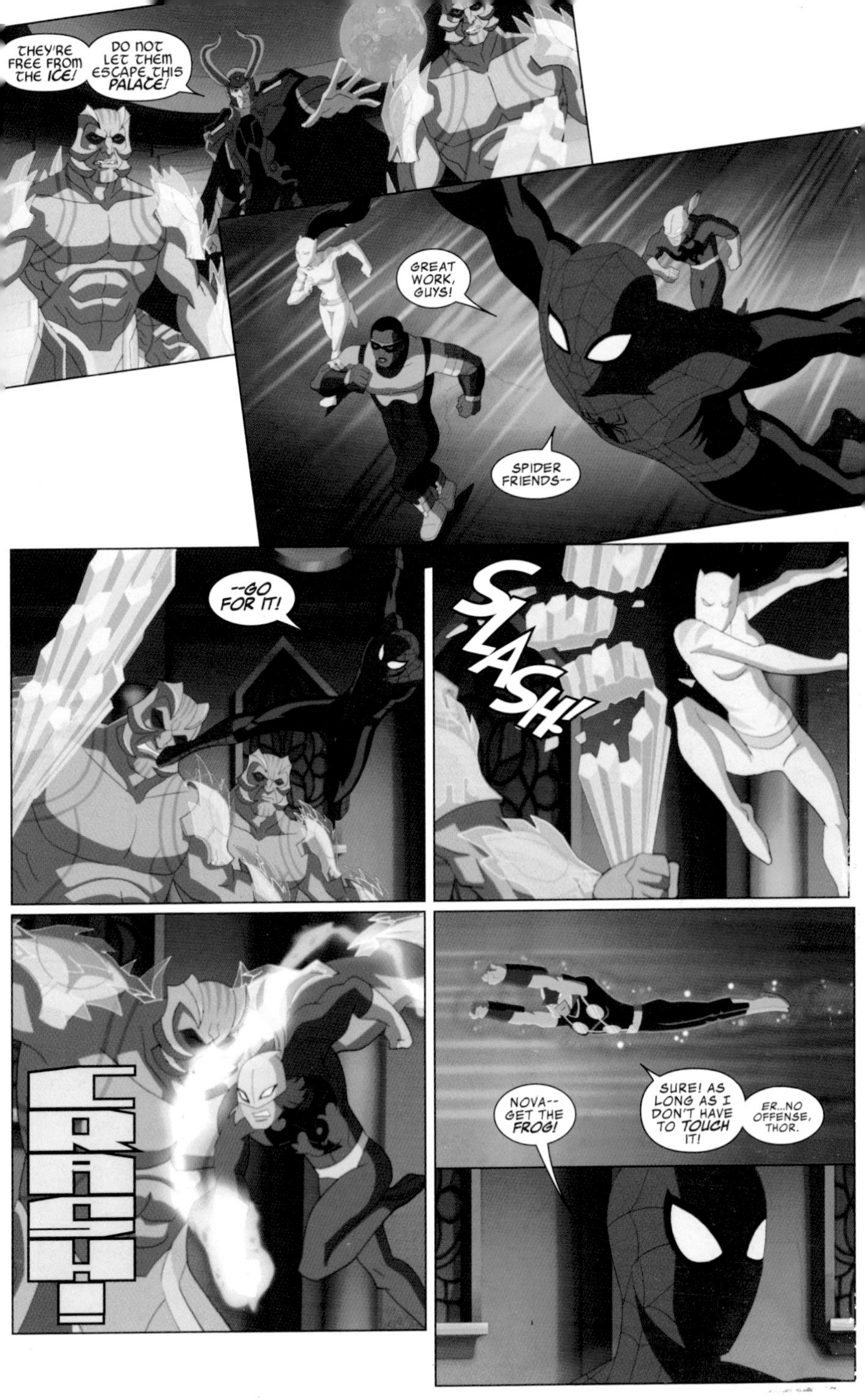
THEY'RE FREE FROM THE ICE!
DO NOT LET THEM ESCAPE THIS PALACE!
GREAT WORK, GUYS!
SPIDER FRIENDS--
--GO FOR IT!
SLASH!
CRASH!
NOVA--GET THE FROG!
SURE! AS LONG AS I DON'T HAVE TO TOUCH IT!
ER...NO OFFENSE, THOR.

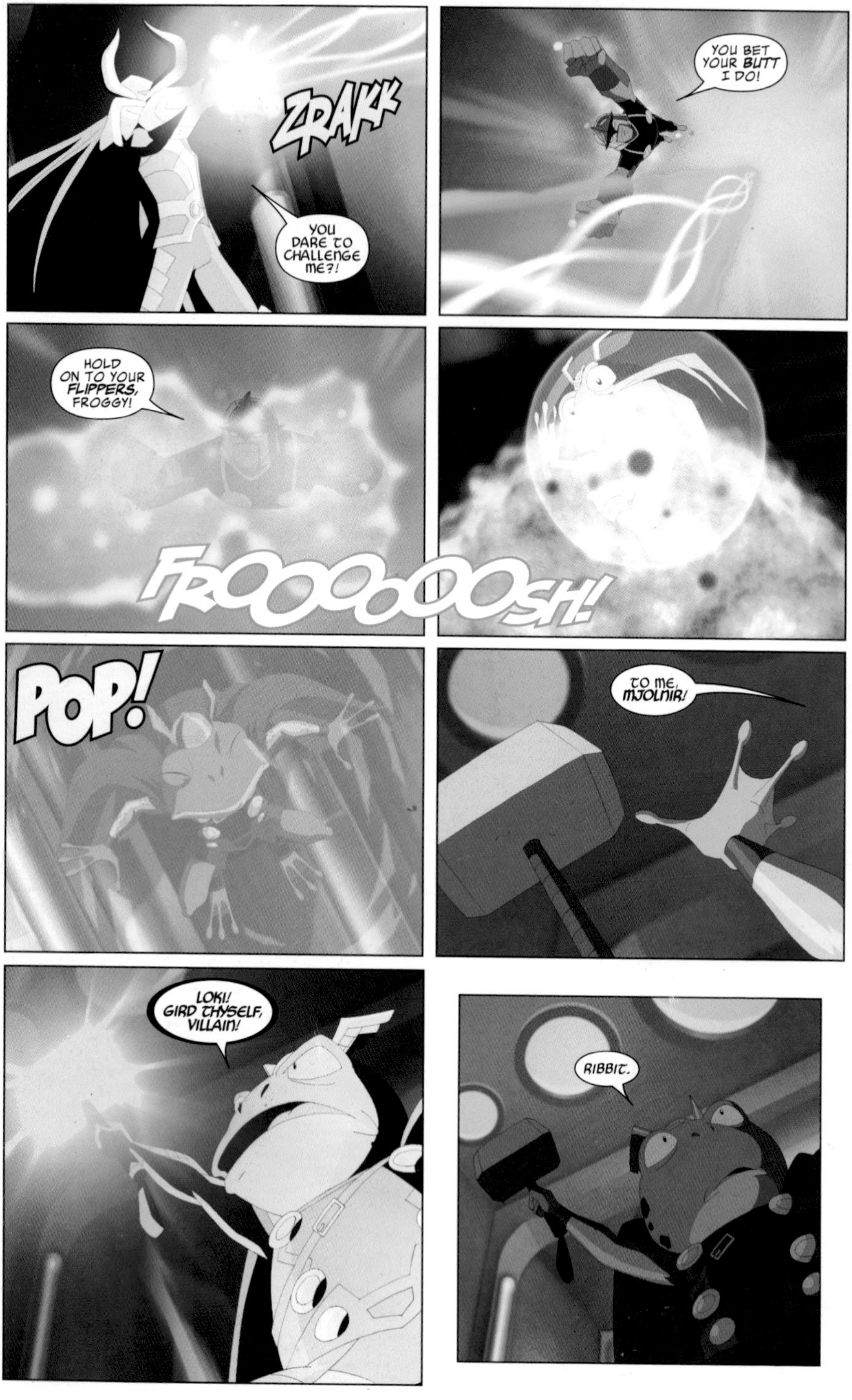
ZRAKK
YOU DARE TO CHALLENGE ME?!
YOU BET YOUR BUTT I DO!
HOLD ON TO YOUR FLIPPERS, FROGGY!
FROOOoOOOSH!
POP!
TO ME, MJOLNIR!
LOKI! GIRD THYSELF, VILLAIN!
RIBBIT.

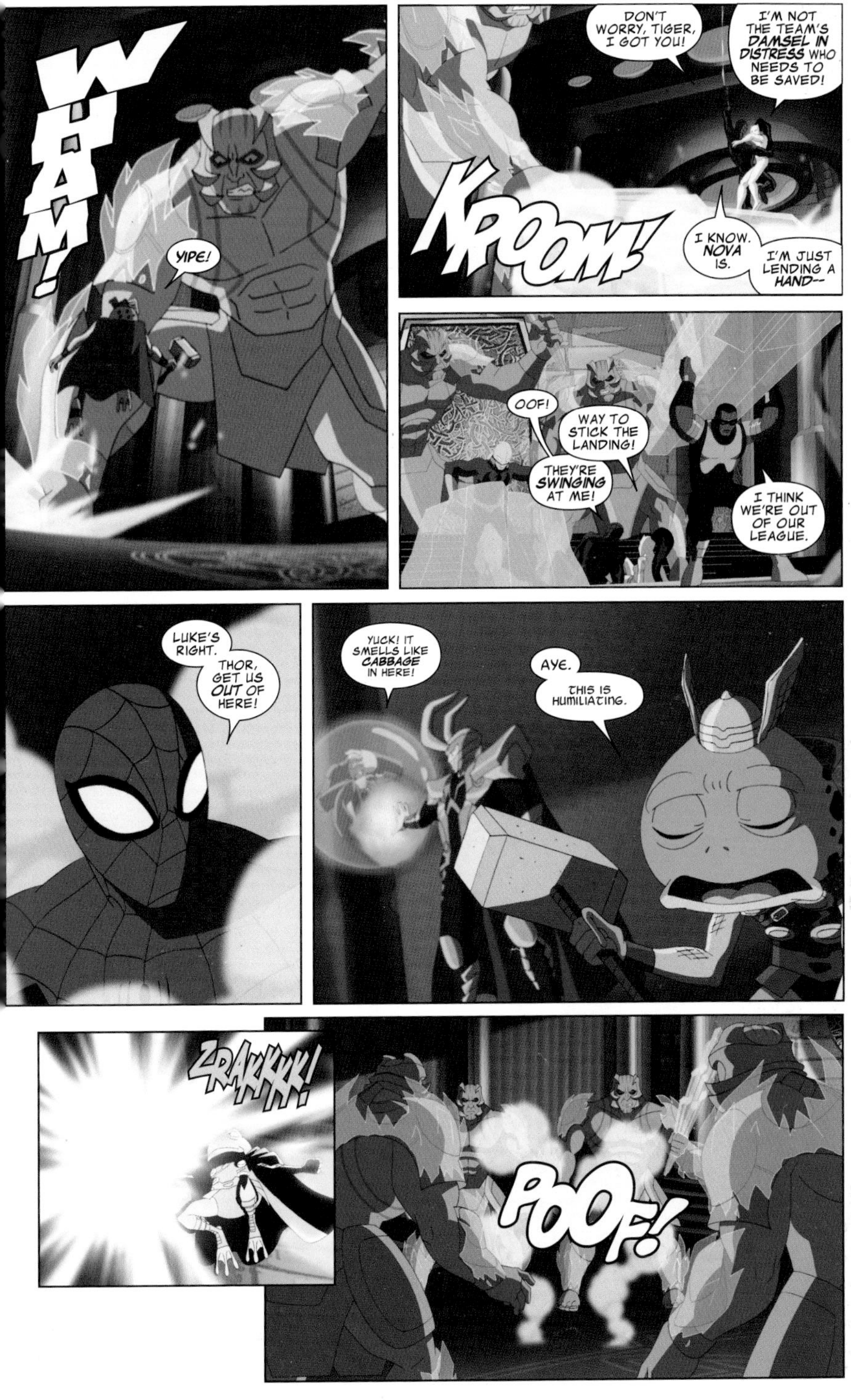
WHAM!
YIPE!
DON'T WORRY, TIGER, I GOT YOU!
I'M NOT THE TEAM'S DAMSEL IN DISTRESS WHO NEEDS TO BE SAVED!
KROOOM!
I KNOW. NOVA IS.
I'M JUST LENDING A HAND--
OOF!
WAY TO STICK THE LANDING!
THEY'RE SWINGING AT ME!
I THINK WE'RE OUT OF OUR LEAGUE.
LUKE'S RIGHT.
THOR, GET US OUT OF HERE!
YUCK! IT SMELLS LIKE CABBAGE IN HERE!
AYE.
THIS IS HUMILIATING.
ZRAKKKK!
POOF!

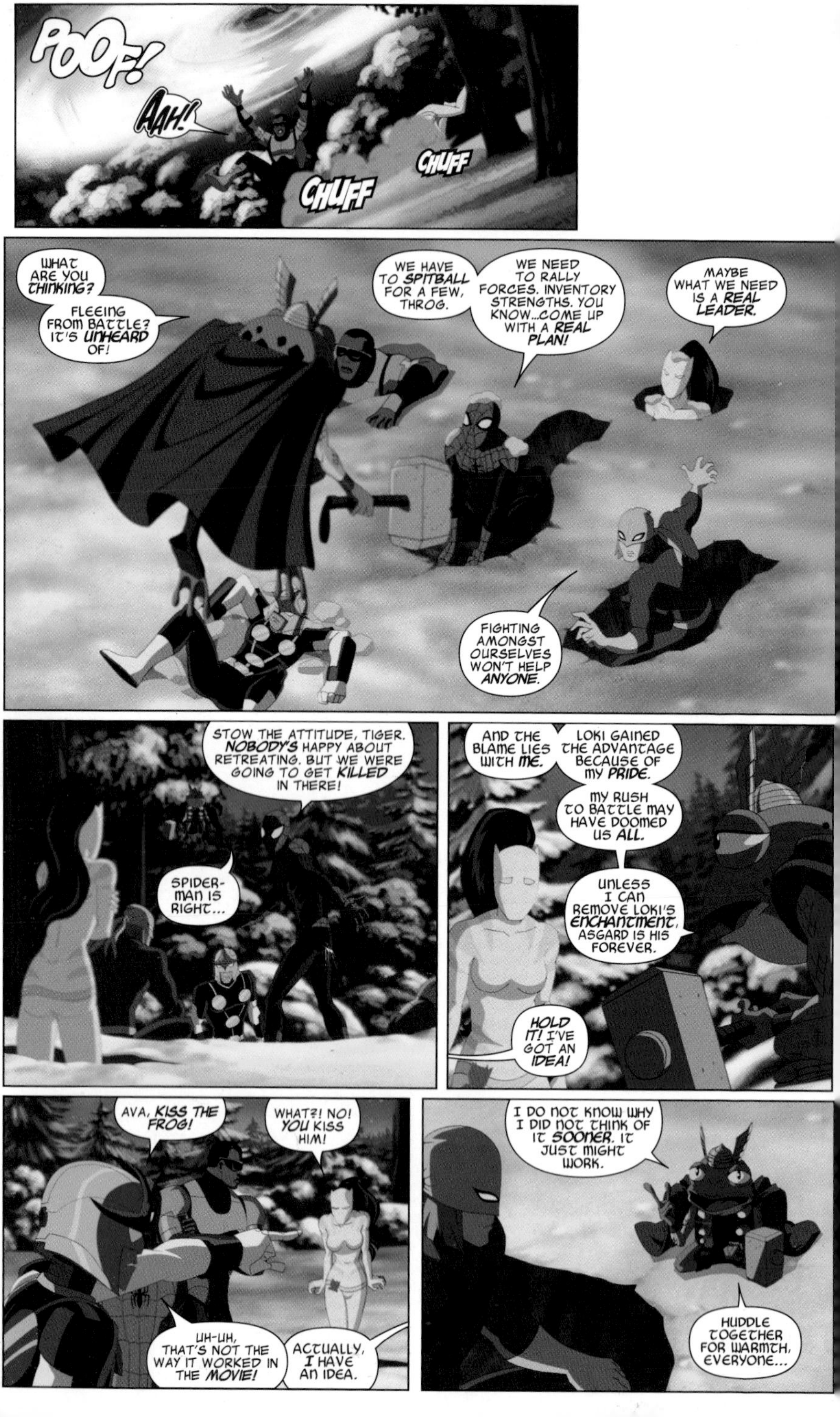
POOF!
AAH!
CHUFF
CHUFF
WHAT ARE YOU THINKING?
FLEEING FROM BATTLE? IT'S UNHEARD OF!
WE HAVE TO SPITBALL FOR A FEW, THROG.
WE NEED TO RALLY FORCES. INVENTORY STRENGTHS. YOU KNOW...COME UP WITH A REAL PLAN!
MAYBE WHAT WE NEED IS A REAL LEADER.
FIGHTING AMONGST OURSELVES WON'T HELP ANYONE.
STOW THE ATTITUDE, TIGER. NOBODY'S HAPPY ABOUT RETREATING. BUT WE WERE GOING TO GET KILLED IN THERE!
SPIDER-MAN IS RIGHT...
AND THE BLAME LIES WITH ME.
LOKI GAINED THE ADVANTAGE BECAUSE OF MY PRIDE.
MY RUSH TO BATTLE MAY HAVE DOOMED US ALL.
UNLESS I CAN REMOVE LOKI'S ENCHANTMENT, ASGARD IS HIS FOREVER.
HOLD IT! I'VE GOT AN IDEA!
AVA, KISS THE FROG!
WHAT?! NO! YOU KISS HIM!
UH-UH, THAT'S NOT THE WAY IT WORKED IN THE MOVIE!
ACTUALLY, I HAVE AN IDEA.
I DO NOT KNOW WHY I DID NOT THINK OF IT SOONER. IT JUST MIGHT WORK.
HUDDLE TOGETHER FOR WARMTH, EVERYONE...

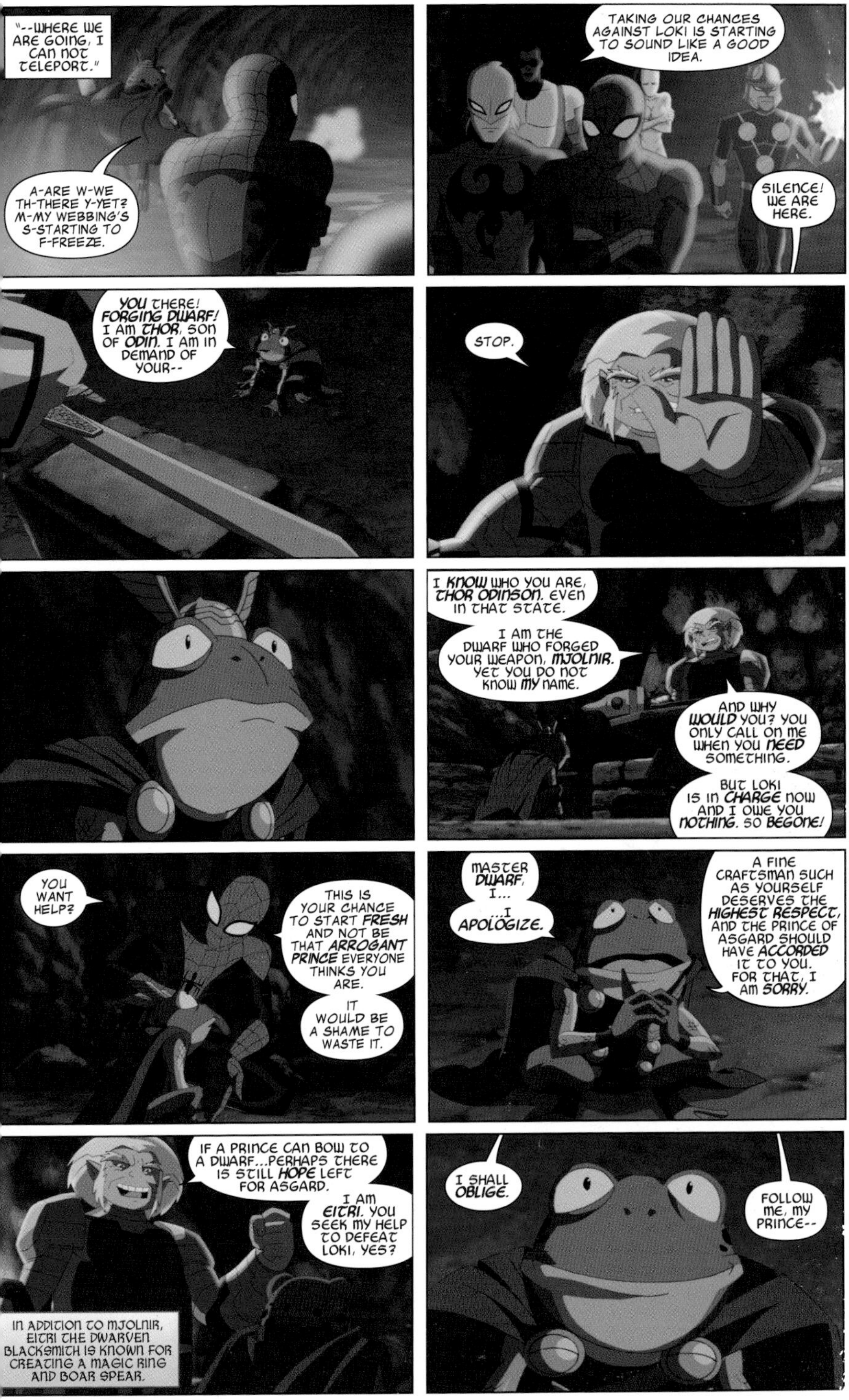
"--WHERE WE ARE GOING, I CAN NOT TELEPORT."
A-ARE W-WE TH-THERE Y-YET? M-MY WEBBING'S S-STARTING TO F-FREEZE.
TAKING OUR CHANCES AGAINST LOKI IS STARTING TO SOUND LIKE A GOOD IDEA.
SILENCE! WE ARE HERE.
YOU THERE! FORGING DWARF! I AM THOR, SON OF ODIN. I AM IN DEMAND OF YOUR--
STOP.
I KNOW WHO YOU ARE, THOR ODINSON. EVEN IN THAT STATE.
I AM THE DWARF WHO FORGED YOUR WEAPON, MJOLNIR. YET YOU DO NOT KNOW MY NAME.
AND WHY WOULD YOU? YOU ONLY CALL ON ME WHEN YOU NEED SOMETHING.
BUT LOKI IS IN CHARGE NOW AND I OWE YOU NOTHING. SO BEGONE!
YOU WANT HELP?
THIS IS YOUR CHANCE TO START FRESH AND NOT BE THAT ARROGANT PRINCE EVERYONE THINKS YOU ARE.
IT WOULD BE A SHAME TO WASTE IT.
MASTER DWARF, I...
...I APOLOGIZE.
A FINE CRAFTSMAN SUCH AS YOURSELF DESERVES THE HIGHEST RESPECT, AND THE PRINCE OF ASGARD SHOULD HAVE ACCORDED IT TO YOU. FOR THAT, I AM SORRY.
IF A PRINCE CAN BOW TO A DWARF...PERHAPS THERE IS STILL HOPE LEFT FOR ASGARD.
I AM EITRI. YOU SEEK MY HELP TO DEFEAT LOKI, YES?
IN ADDITION TO MJOLNIR, EITRI THE DWARVEN BLACKSMITH IS KNOWN FOR CREATING A MAGIC RING AND BOAR SPEAR.
I SHALL OBLIGE.
FOLLOW ME, MY PRINCE--

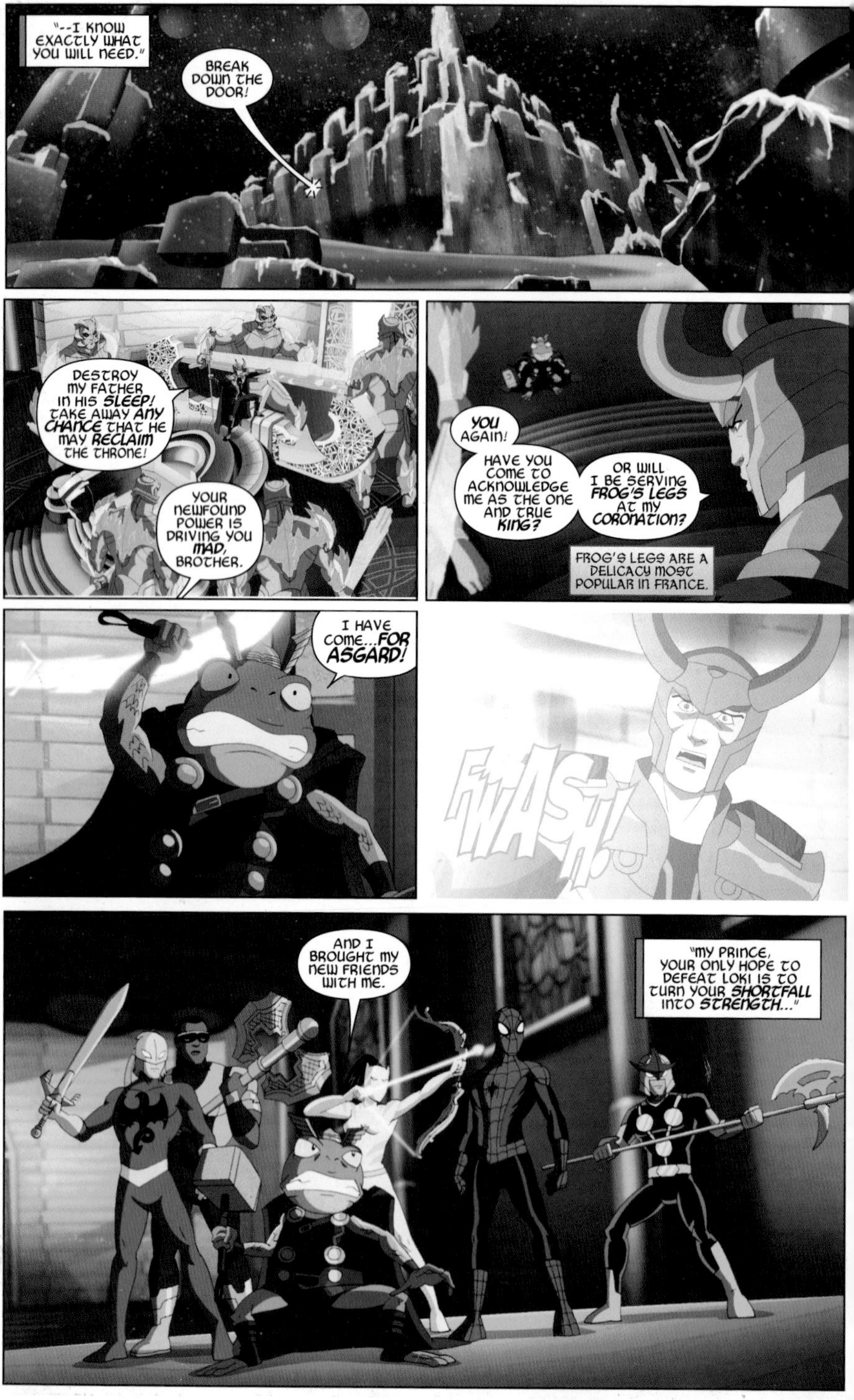
"--I KNOW EXACTLY WHAT YOU WILL NEED."
BREAK DOWN THE DOOR!
DESTROY MY FATHER IN HIS SLEEP! TAKE AWAY ANY CHANCE THAT HE MAY RECLAIM THE THRONE!
YOUR NEWFOUND POWER IS DRIVING YOU MAD, BROTHER.
YOU AGAIN!
HAVE YOU COME TO ACKNOWLEDGE ME AS THE ONE AND TRUE KING?
OR WILL I BE SERVING FROG'S LEGS AT MY CORONATION?
FROG'S LEGS ARE A DELICACY MOST POPULAR IN FRANCE.
I HAVE COME...FOR ASGARD!
FWASH!
AND I BROUGHT MY NEW FRIENDS WITH ME.
"MY PRINCE, YOUR ONLY HOPE TO DEFEAT LOKI IS TO TURN YOUR SHORTFALL INTO STRENGTH..."

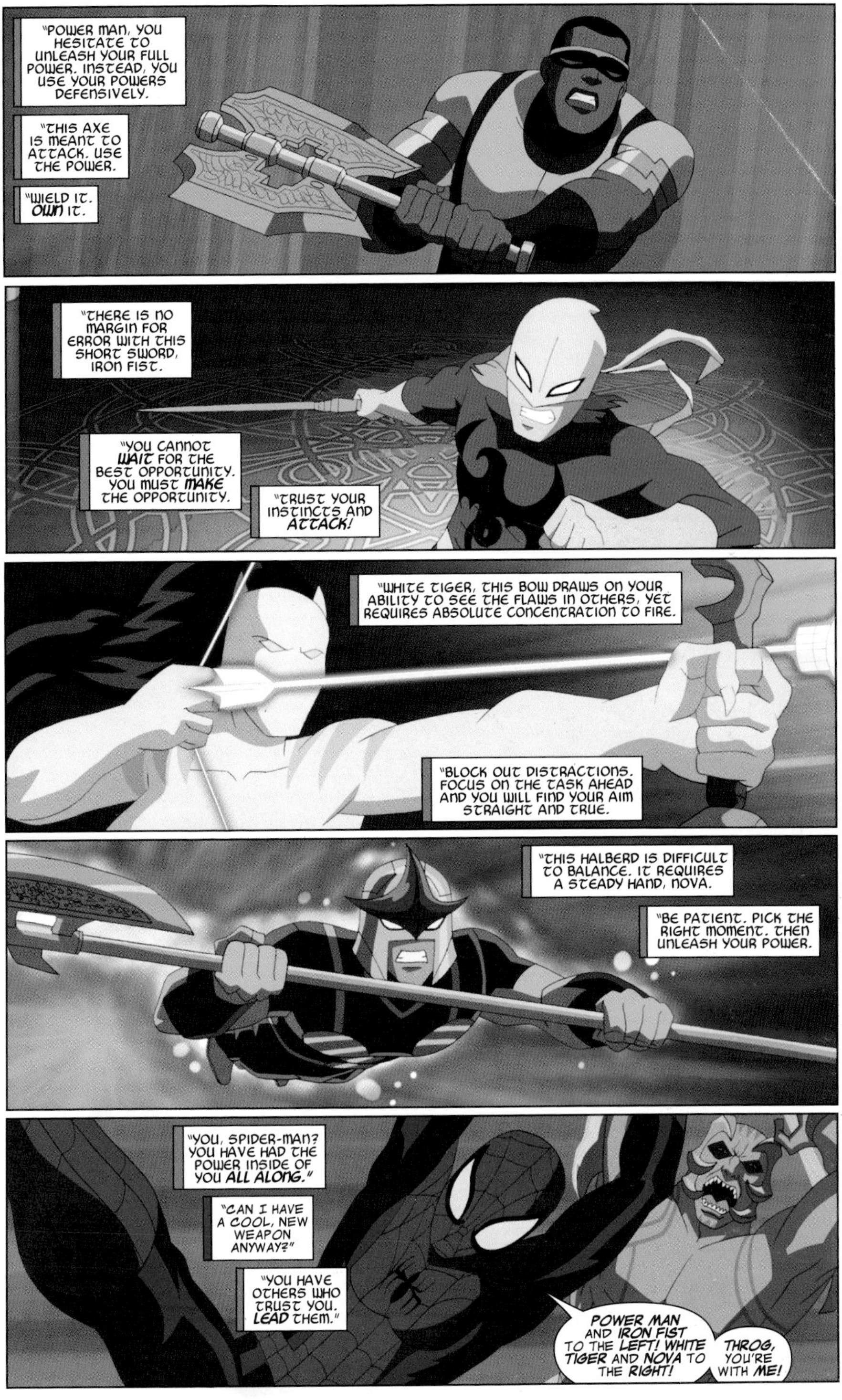
"POWER MAN, YOU HESITATE TO UNLEASH YOUR FULL POWER. INSTEAD, YOU USE YOUR POWERS DEFENSIVELY.
"THIS AXE IS MEANT TO ATTACK. USE THE POWER.
"WIELD IT. OWN IT.
"THERE IS NO MARGIN FOR ERROR WITH THIS SHORT SWORD, IRON FIST.
"YOU CANNOT WAIT FOR THE BEST OPPORTUNITY. YOU MUST MAKE THE OPPORTUNITY.
"TRUST YOUR INSTINCTS AND ATTACK!
"WHITE TIGER, THIS BOW DRAWS ON YOUR ABILITY TO SEE THE FLAWS IN OTHERS, YET REQUIRES ABSOLUTE CONCENTRATION TO FIRE.
"BLOCK OUT DISTRACTIONS. FOCUS ON THE TASK AHEAD AND YOU WILL FIND YOUR AIM STRAIGHT AND TRUE.
"THIS HALBERD IS DIFFICULT TO BALANCE. IT REQUIRES A STEADY HAND, NOVA.
"BE PATIENT. PICK THE RIGHT MOMENT. THEN UNLEASH YOUR POWER.
"YOU, SPIDER-MAN? YOU HAVE HAD THE POWER INSIDE OF YOU ALL ALONG."
"CAN I HAVE A COOL, NEW WEAPON ANYWAY?"
"YOU HAVE OTHERS WHO TRUST YOU. LEAD THEM."
POWER MAN AND IRON FIST TO THE LEFT! WHITE TIGER AND NOVA TO THE RIGHT!
THROG, YOU'RE WITH ME!

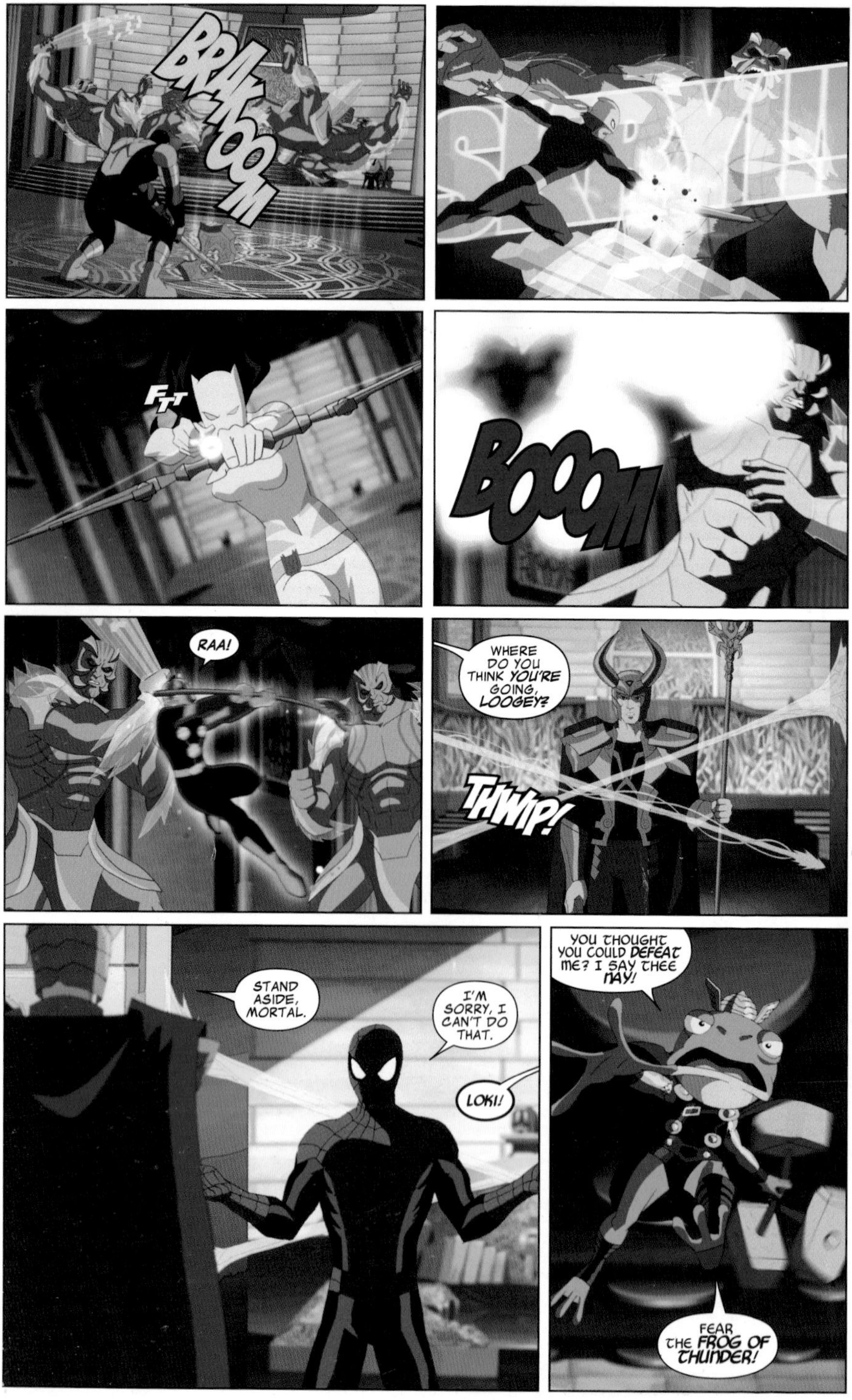
BRAKOOM
FTT
BOOOM
RAA!
WHERE DO YOU THINK YOU'RE GOING, LOOGEY?
THWIP!
STAND ASIDE, MORTAL.
I'M SORRY, I CAN'T DO THAT.
LOKI!
YOU THOUGHT YOU COULD DEFEAT ME? I SAY THEE NAY!
FEAR THE FROG OF THUNDER!

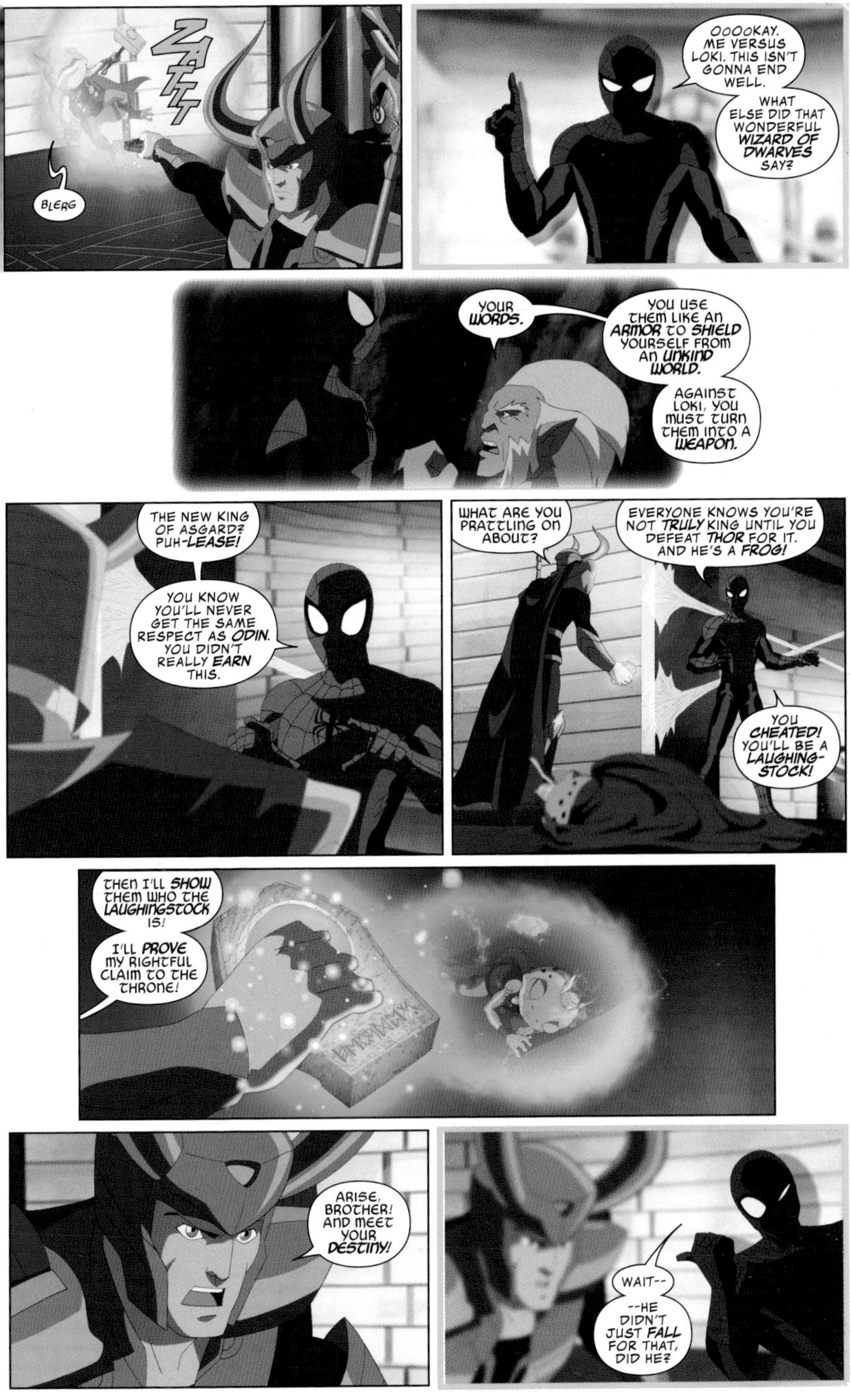

ZATT
BLERG
OOOOKAY. ME VERSUS LOKI. THIS ISN'T GONNA END WELL.
WHAT ELSE DID THAT WONDERFUL WIZARD OF DWARVES SAY?
YOUR WORDS.
YOU USE THEM LIKE AN ARMOR TO SHIELD YOURSELF FROM AN UNKIND WORLD.
AGAINST LOKI, YOU MUST TURN THEM INTO A WEAPON.
THE NEW KING OF ASGARD? PUH-LEASE!
YOU KNOW YOU'LL NEVER GET THE SAME RESPECT AS ODIN. YOU DIDN'T REALLY EARN THIS.
WHAT ARE YOU PRATTLING ON ABOUT?
EVERYONE KNOWS YOU'RE NOT TRULY KING UNTIL YOU DEFEAT THOR FOR IT. AND HE'S A FROG!
YOU CHEATED! YOU'LL BE A LAUGHING-STOCK!
THEN I'LL SHOW THEM WHO THE LAUGHINGSTOCK IS!
I'LL PROVE MY RIGHTFUL CLAIM TO THE THRONE!
ARISE, BROTHER! AND MEET YOUR DESTINY!
WAIT--
--HE DIDN'T JUST FALL FOR THAT, DID HE?

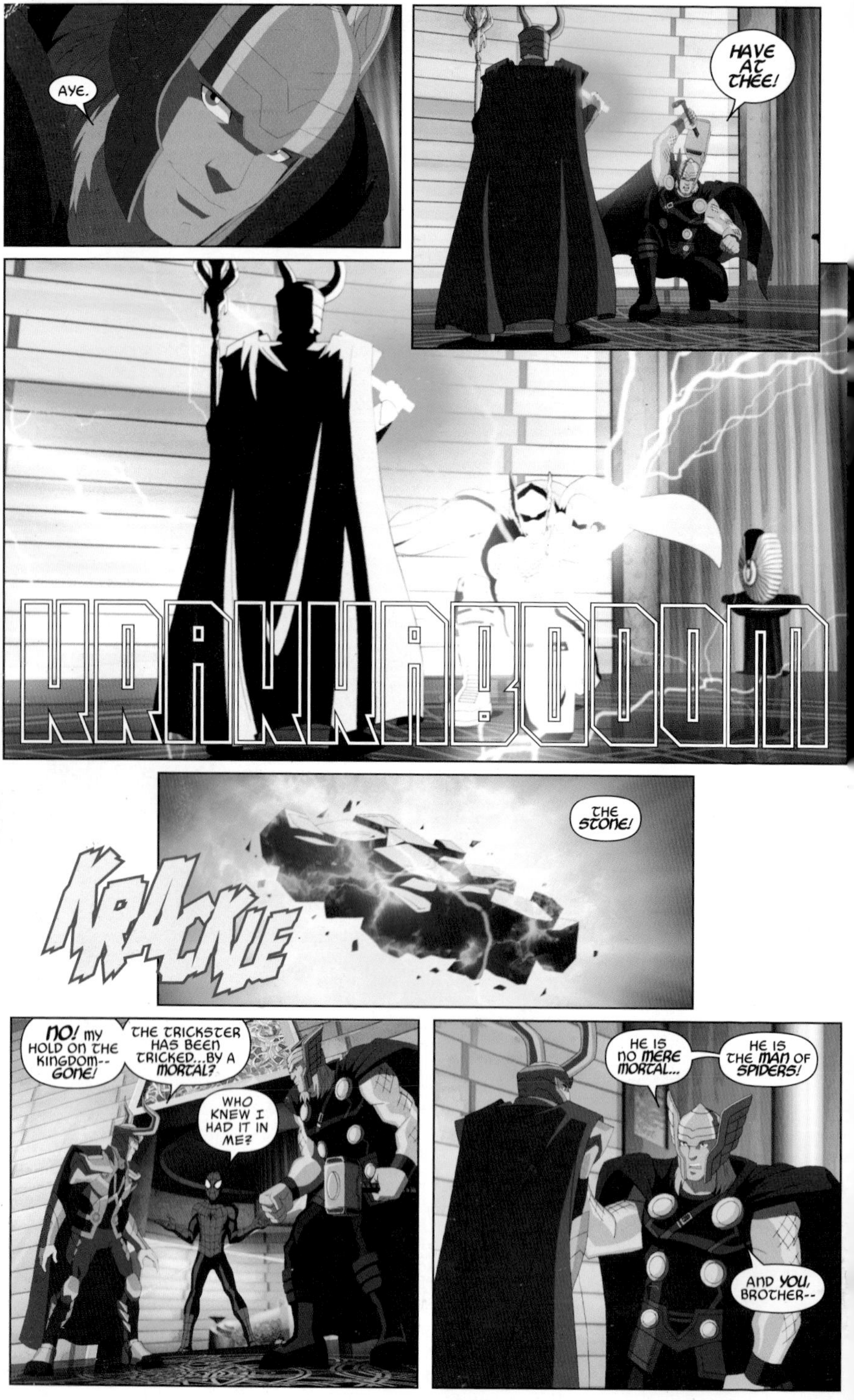

AYE.
HAVE AT THEE!
KRAKKA-BOOM
KRACKLE
THE STONE!
NO! MY HOLD ON THE KINGDOM--GONE!
THE TRICKSTER HAS BEEN TRICKED...BY A MORTAL?
WHO KNEW I HAD IT IN ME?
HE IS NO MERE MORTAL...
HE IS THE MAN OF SPIDERS!
AND YOU, BROTHER--

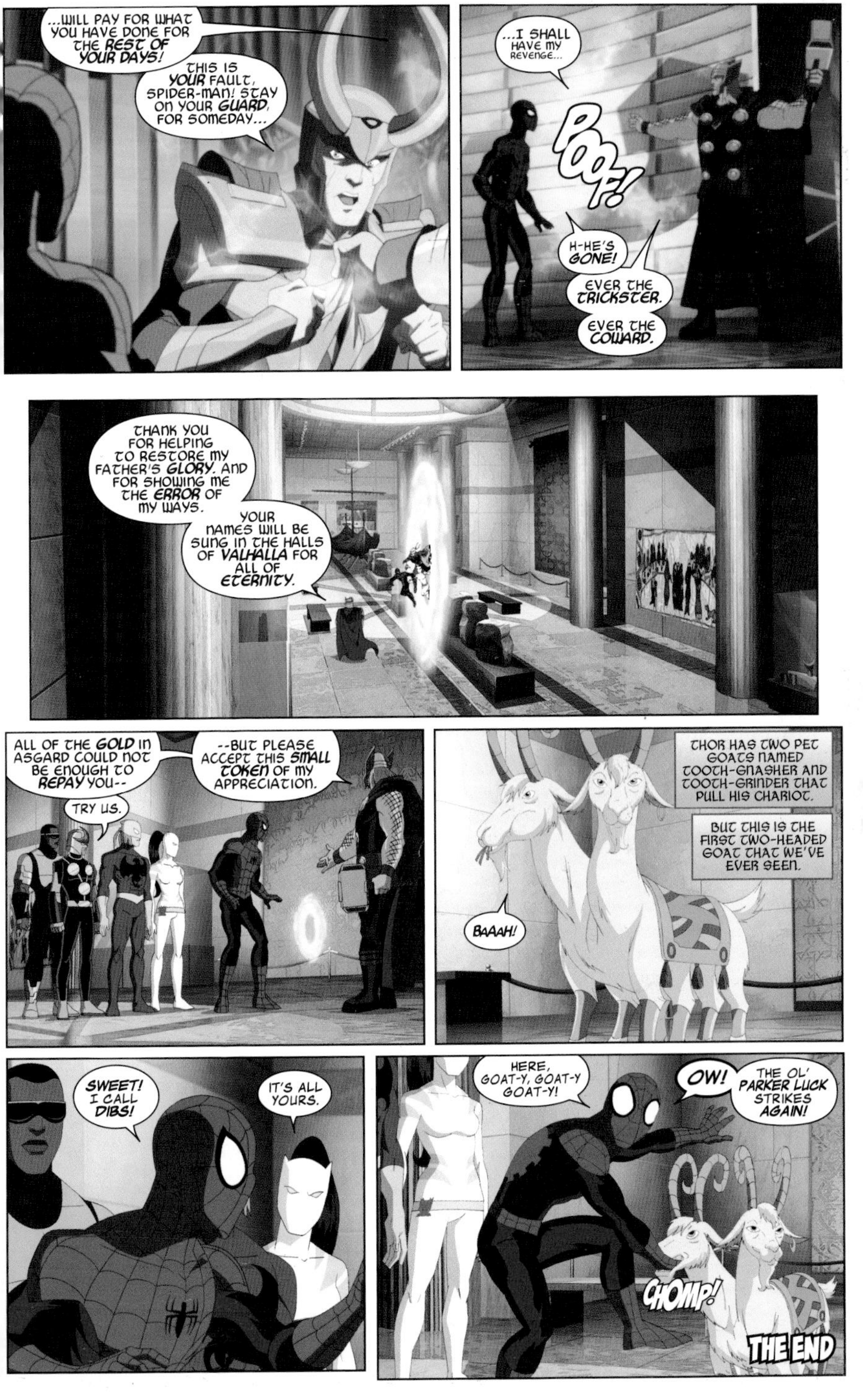
...WILL PAY FOR WHAT YOU HAVE DONE FOR THE REST OF YOUR DAYS!
THIS IS YOUR FAULT, SPIDER-MAN! STAY ON YOUR GUARD, FOR SOMEDAY...
...I SHALL HAVE MY REVENGE...
POOF!
H-HE'S GONE!
EVER THE TRICKSTER.
EVER THE COWARD.
THANK YOU FOR HELPING TO RESTORE MY FATHER'S GLORY. AND FOR SHOWING ME THE ERROR OF MY WAYS.
YOUR NAMES WILL BE SUNG IN THE HALLS OF VALHALLA FOR ALL OF ETERNITY.
ALL OF THE GOLD IN ASGARD COULD NOT BE ENOUGH TO REPAY YOU--
--BUT PLEASE ACCEPT THIS SMALL TOKEN OF MY APPRECIATION.
TRY US.
THOR HAS TWO PET GOATS NAMED TOOTH-GNASHER AND TOOTH-GRINDER THAT PULL HIS CHARIOT.
BUT THIS IS THE FIRST TWO-HEADED GOAT THAT WE'VE EVER SEEN.
BAAAH!
SWEET! I CALL DIBS!
IT'S ALL YOURS.
HERE, GOAT-Y, GOAT-Y GOAT-Y!
OW!
THE OL' PARKER LUCK STRIKES AGAIN!
CHOMP!
THE END

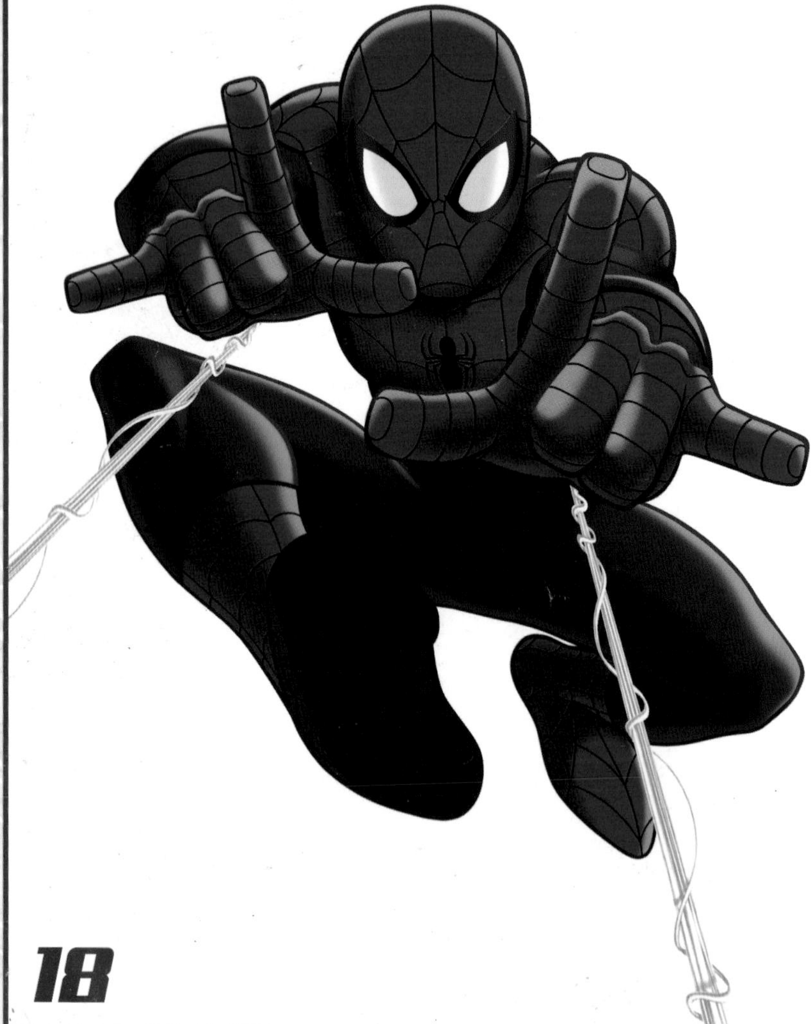

18

Based on **"Freaky"**

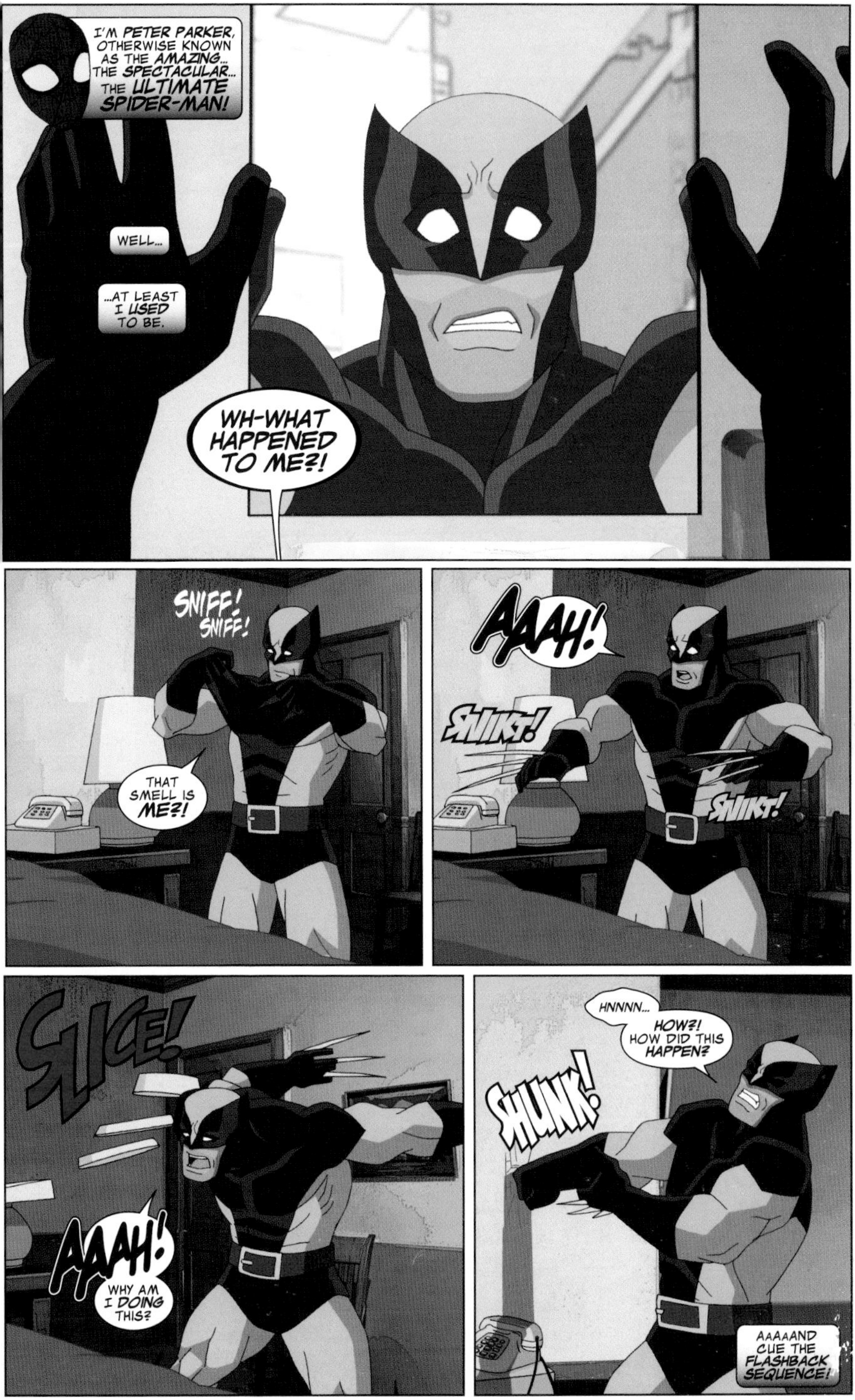
I'M PETER PARKER, OTHERWISE KNOWN AS THE AMAZING... THE SPECTACULAR... THE ULTIMATE SPIDER-MAN!
WELL...
...AT LEAST I USED TO BE.
WH-WHAT HAPPENED TO ME?!
SNIFF! SNIFF!
THAT SMELL IS ME?!
AAAH!
SNIKT!
SNIKT!
SLICE!
AAAH!
WHY AM I DOING THIS?
HNNNN... HOW?! HOW DID THIS HAPPEN?
SHUNK!
AAAAAND CUE THE FLASHBACK SEQUENCE!

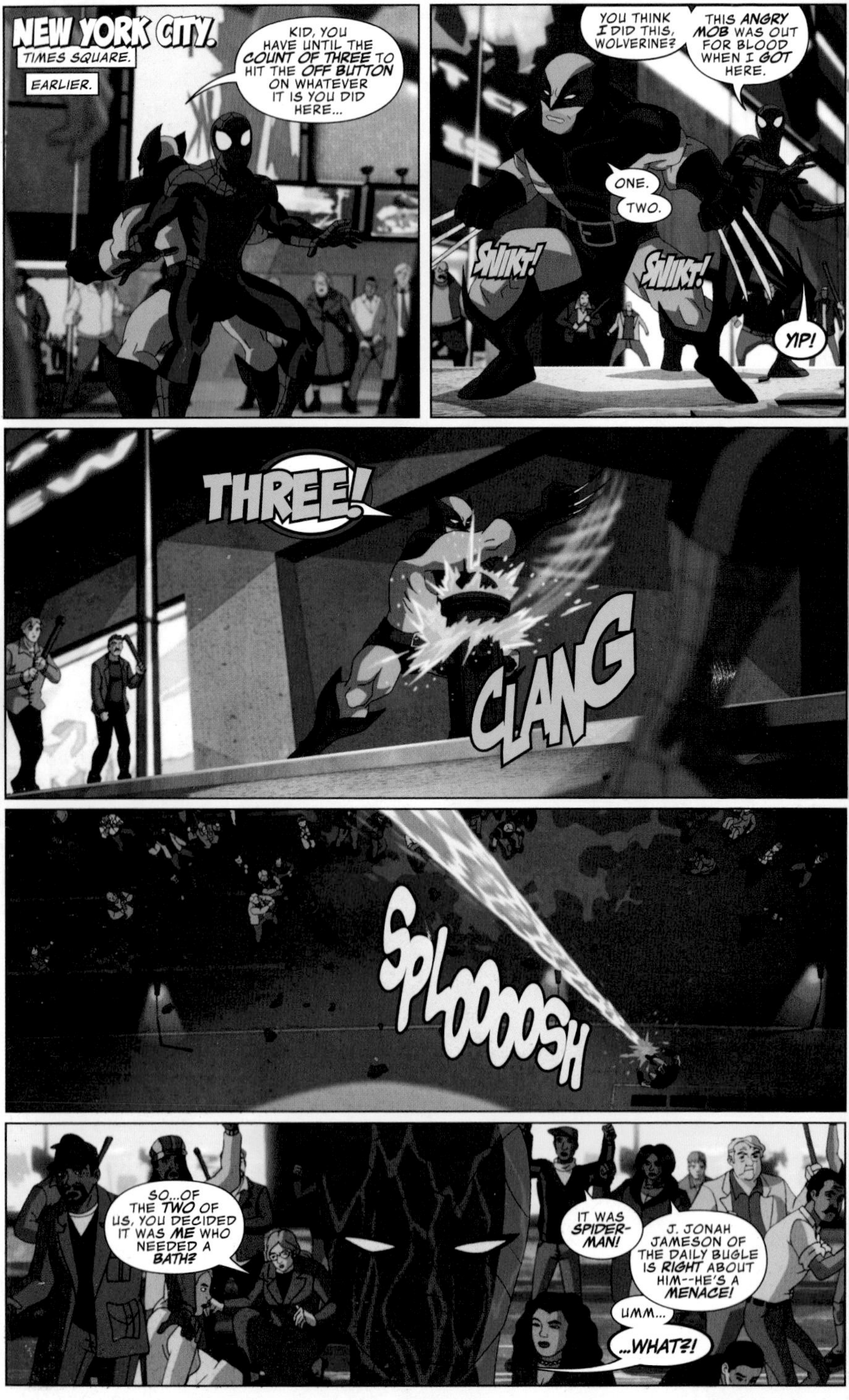
NEW YORK CITY.
TIMES SQUARE.
EARLIER.
KID, YOU HAVE UNTIL THE COUNT OF THREE TO HIT THE OFF BUTTON ON WHATEVER IT IS YOU DID HERE...
YOU THINK I DID THIS, WOLVERINE?
THIS ANGRY MOB WAS OUT FOR BLOOD WHEN I GOT HERE.
ONE.
TWO.
SNIKT!
SNIKT!
YIP!
THREE!
CLANG
SPLOOOOSH
SO...OF THE TWO OF US, YOU DECIDED IT WAS ME WHO NEEDED A BATH?
IT WAS SPIDER-MAN!
J. JONAH JAMESON OF THE DAILY BUGLE IS RIGHT ABOUT HIM--HE'S A MENACE!
UMM...
...WHAT?!

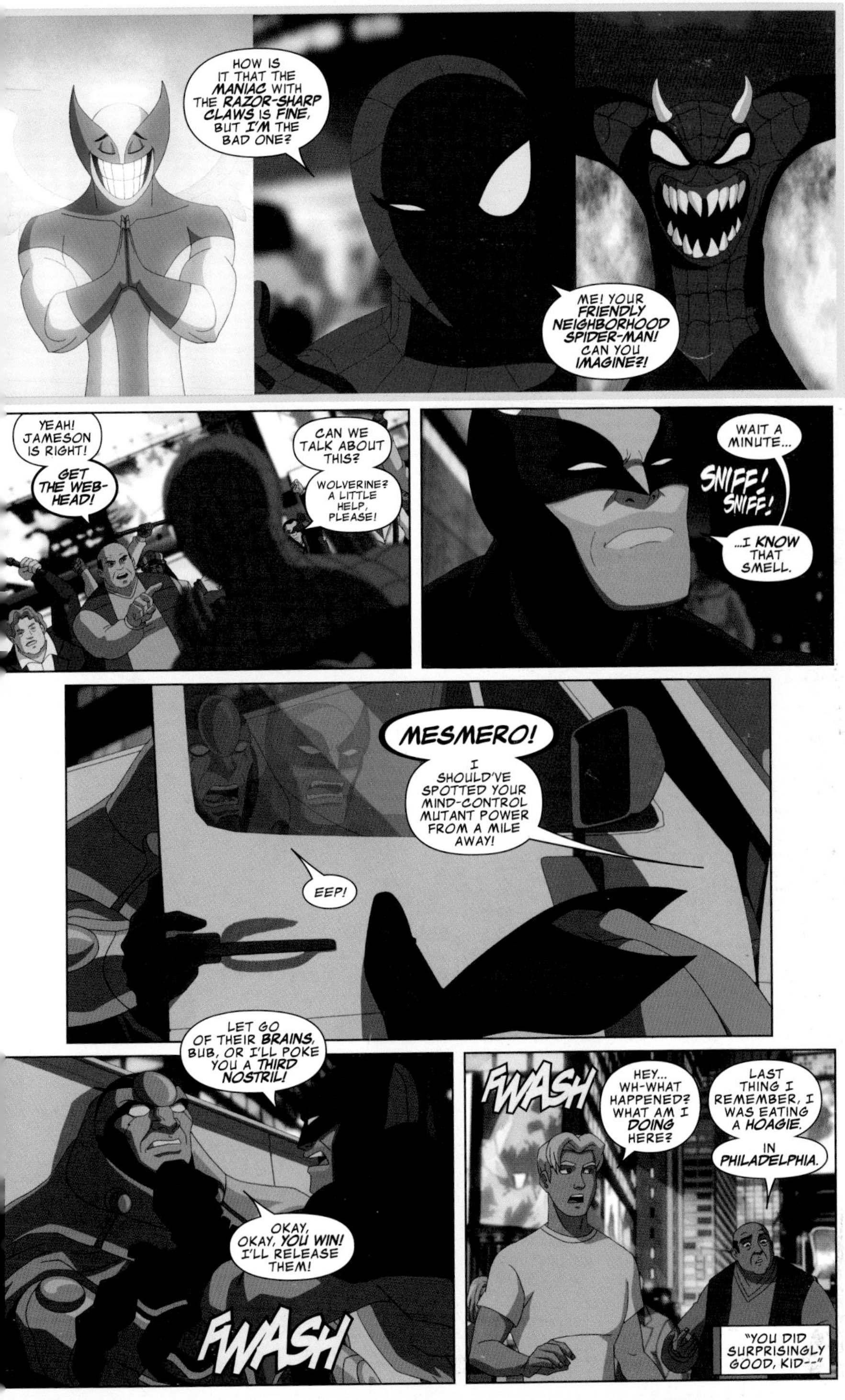

HOW IS IT THAT THE MANIAC WITH THE RAZOR-SHARP CLAWS IS FINE, BUT I'M THE BAD ONE?
ME! YOUR FRIENDLY NEIGHBORHOOD SPIDER-MAN! CAN YOU IMAGINE?!
YEAH! JAMESON IS RIGHT!
GET THE WEB-HEAD!
CAN WE TALK ABOUT THIS?
WOLVERINE? A LITTLE HELP, PLEASE!
WAIT A MINUTE...
SNIFF! SNIFF!
...I KNOW THAT SMELL.
MESMERO!
I SHOULD'VE SPOTTED YOUR MIND-CONTROL MUTANT POWER FROM A MILE AWAY!
EEP!
LET GO OF THEIR BRAINS, BUB, OR I'LL POKE YOU A THIRD NOSTRIL!
OKAY, OKAY, YOU WIN! I'LL RELEASE THEM!
FWASH
FWASH
HEY... WH-WHAT HAPPENED? WHAT AM I DOING HERE?
LAST THING I REMEMBER, I WAS EATING A HOAGIE.
IN PHILADELPHIA.
"YOU DID SURPRISINGLY GOOD, KID--"

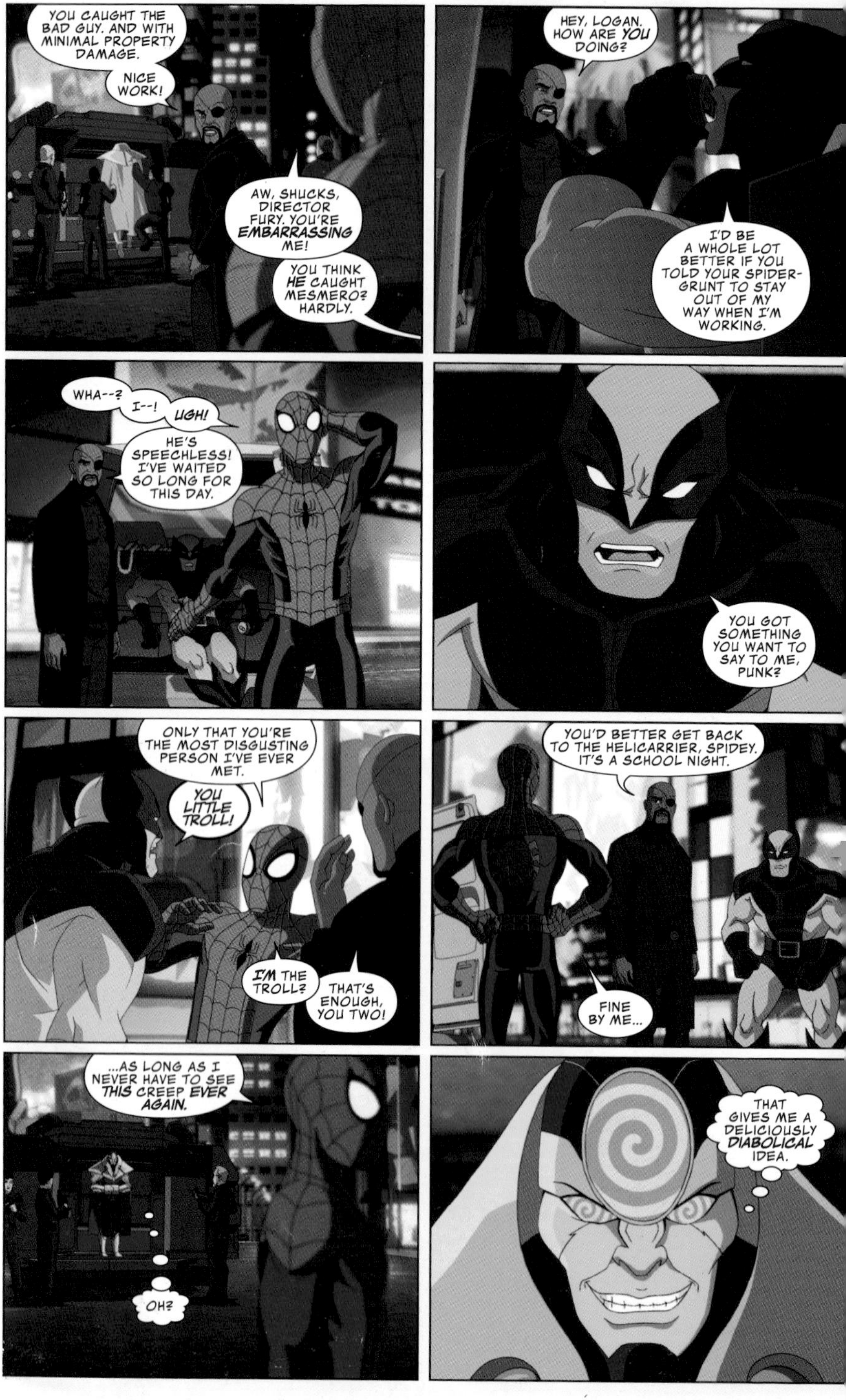
YOU CAUGHT THE BAD GUY. AND WITH MINIMAL PROPERTY DAMAGE.
NICE WORK!
AW, SHUCKS, DIRECTOR FURY. YOU'RE EMBARRASSING ME!
YOU THINK HE CAUGHT MESMERO? HARDLY.
HEY, LOGAN. HOW ARE YOU DOING?
I'D BE A WHOLE LOT BETTER IF YOU TOLD YOUR SPIDER-GRUNT TO STAY OUT OF MY WAY WHEN I'M WORKING.
WHA--?
I--!
UGH!
HE'S SPEECHLESS! I'VE WAITED SO LONG FOR THIS DAY.
YOU GOT SOMETHING YOU WANT TO SAY TO ME, PUNK?
ONLY THAT YOU'RE THE MOST DISGUSTING PERSON I'VE EVER MET.
YOU LITTLE TROLL!
I'M THE TROLL?
THAT'S ENOUGH, YOU TWO!
YOU'D BETTER GET BACK TO THE HELICARRIER, SPIDEY. IT'S A SCHOOL NIGHT.
FINE BY ME...
...AS LONG AS I NEVER HAVE TO SEE THIS CREEP EVER AGAIN.
OH?
THAT GIVES ME A DELICIOUSLY DIABOLICAL IDEA.

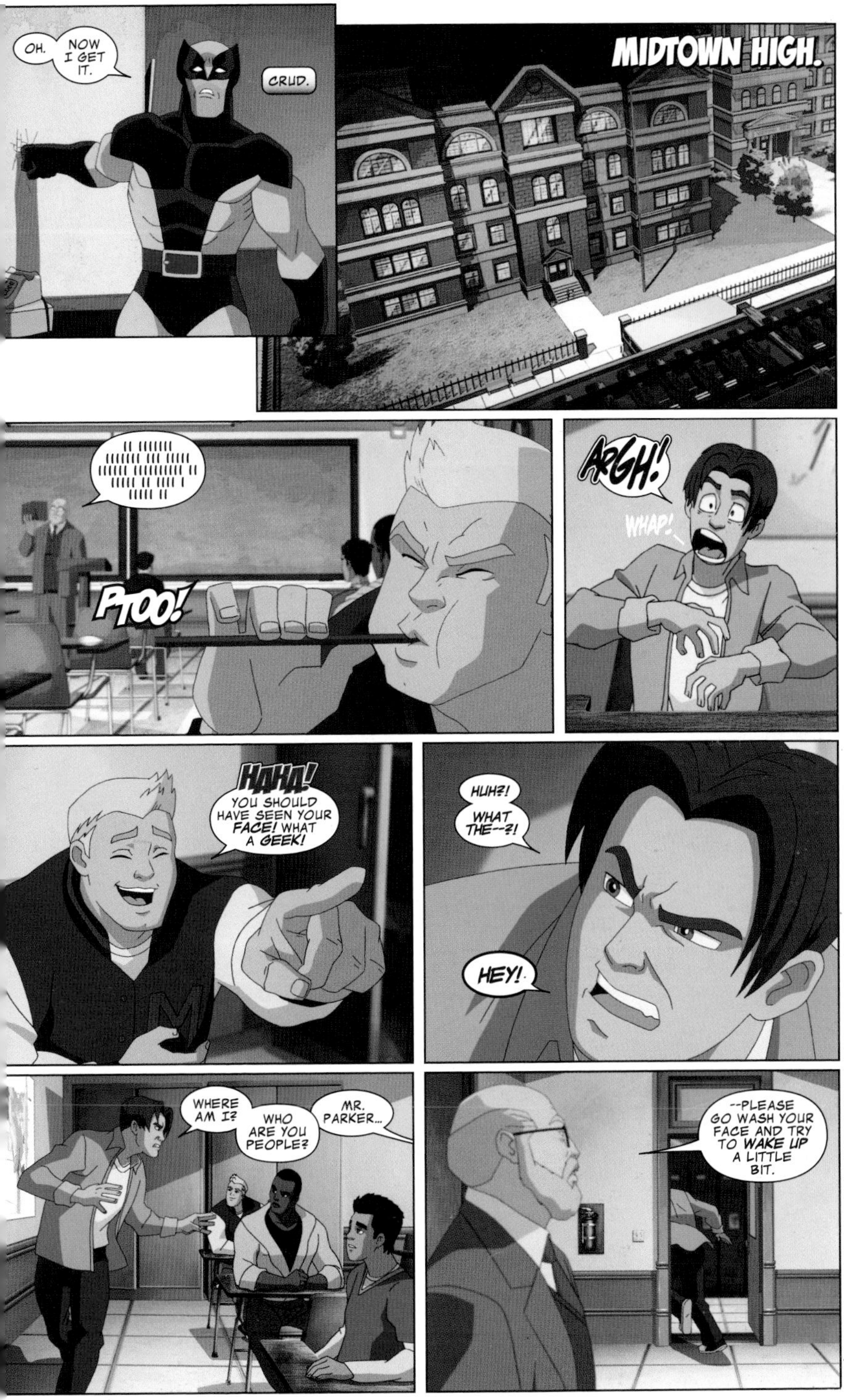
OH.
NOW I GET IT.
CRUD.
MIDTOWN HIGH.
ARGH!
WHAP!
PTOO!
HAHA!
YOU SHOULD HAVE SEEN YOUR FACE! WHAT A GEEK!
HUH?!
WHAT THE--?!
HEY!
WHERE AM I?
WHO ARE YOU PEOPLE?
MR. PARKER...
--PLEASE GO WASH YOUR FACE AND TRY TO WAKE UP A LITTLE BIT.

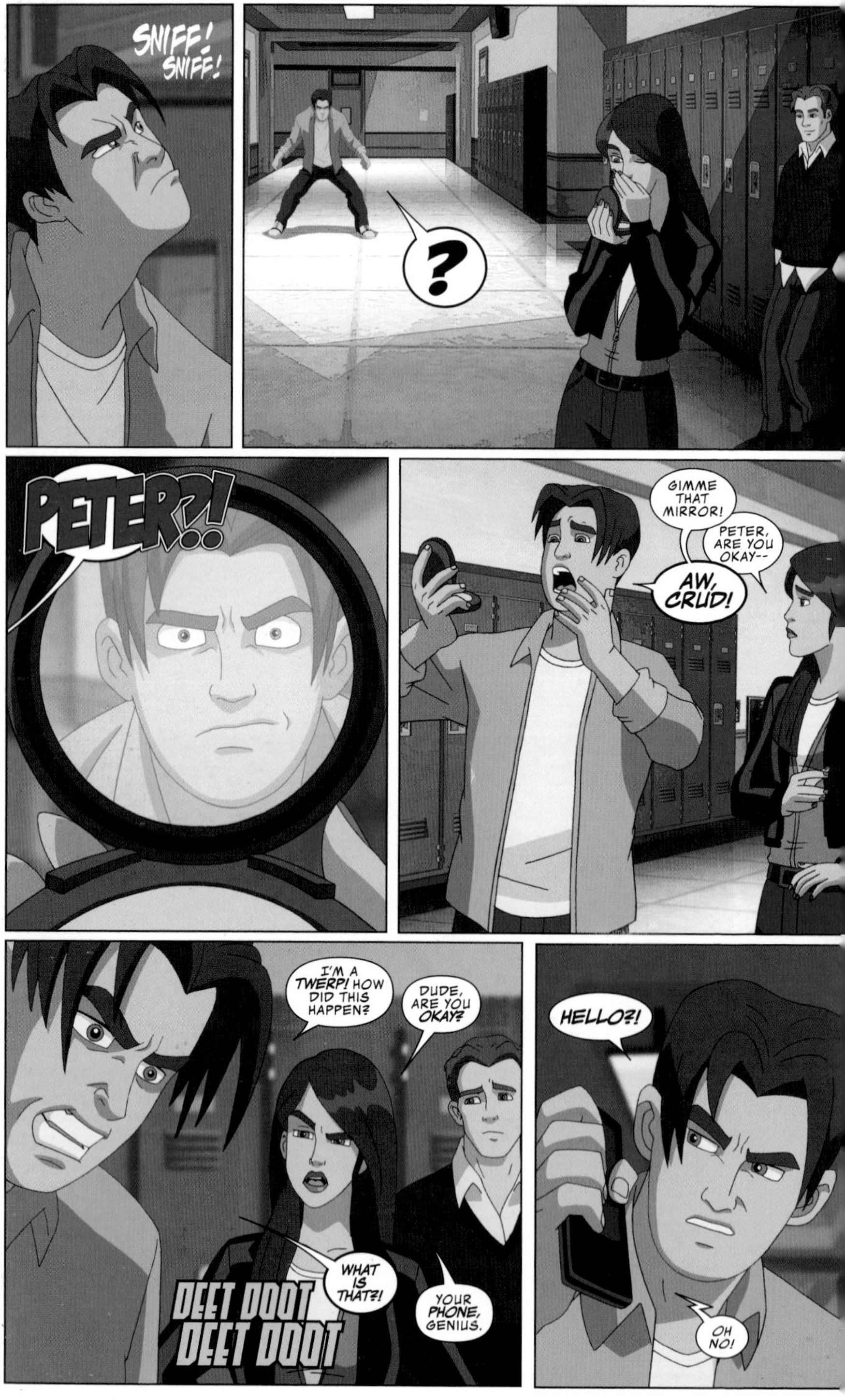
SNIFF! SNIFF!
?
PETER?!
GIMME THAT MIRROR!
PETER, ARE YOU OKAY--
AW, CRUD!
I'M A TWERP! HOW DID THIS HAPPEN?
DUDE, ARE YOU OKAY?
DEET DOOT DEET DOOT
WHAT IS THAT?!
YOUR PHONE, GENIUS.
HELLO?!
OH NO!

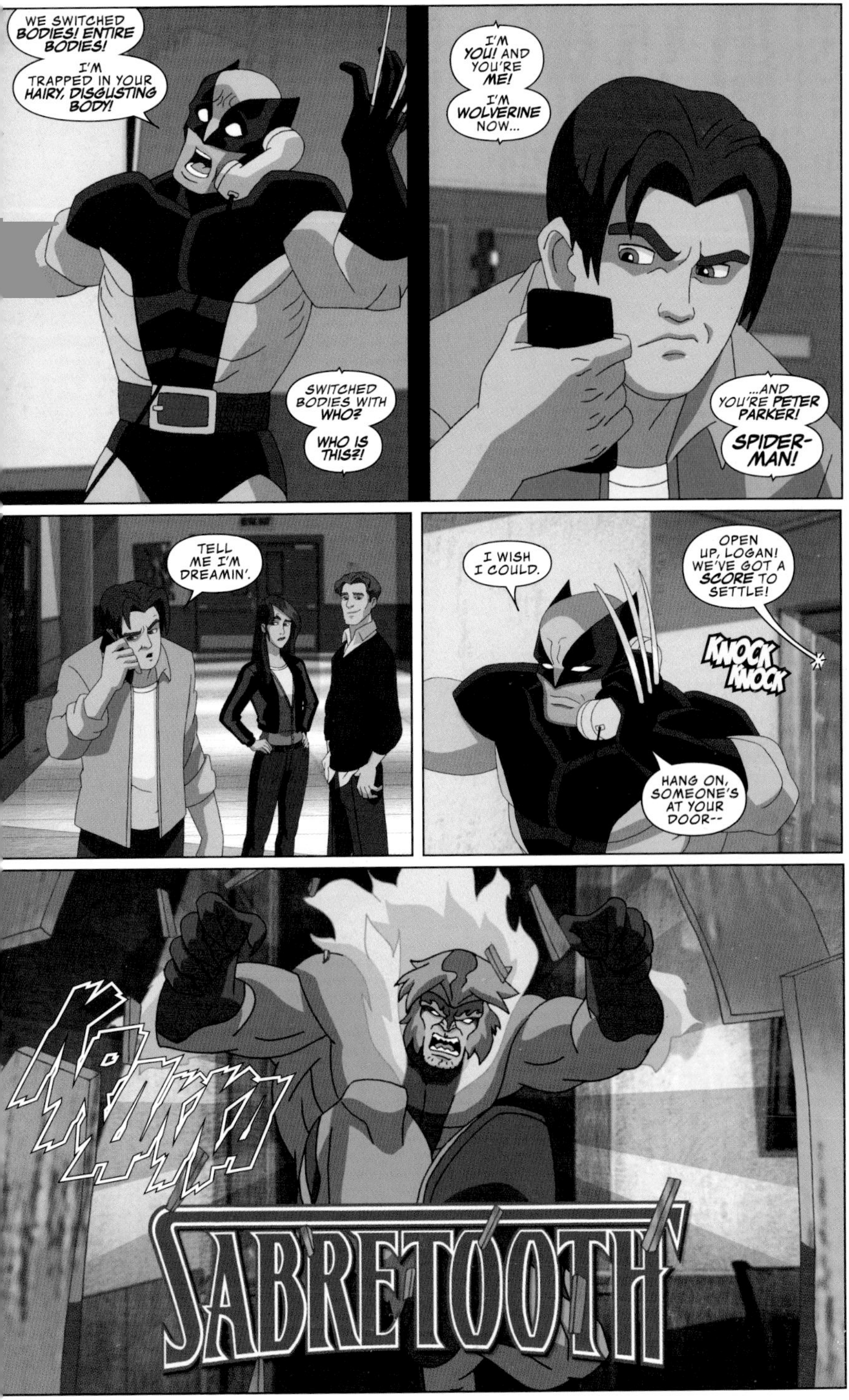

WE SWITCHED BODIES! ENTIRE BODIES!
I'M TRAPPED IN YOUR HAIRY, DISGUSTING BODY!
SWITCHED BODIES WITH WHO?
WHO IS THIS?!
I'M YOU! AND YOU'RE ME!
I'M WOLVERINE NOW...
...AND YOU'RE PETER PARKER!
SPIDER-MAN!
TELL ME I'M DREAMIN'.
I WISH I COULD.
OPEN UP, LOGAN! WE'VE GOT A SCORE TO SETTLE!
KNOCK KNOCK
HANG ON, SOMEONE'S AT YOUR DOOR--
SABRETOOTH

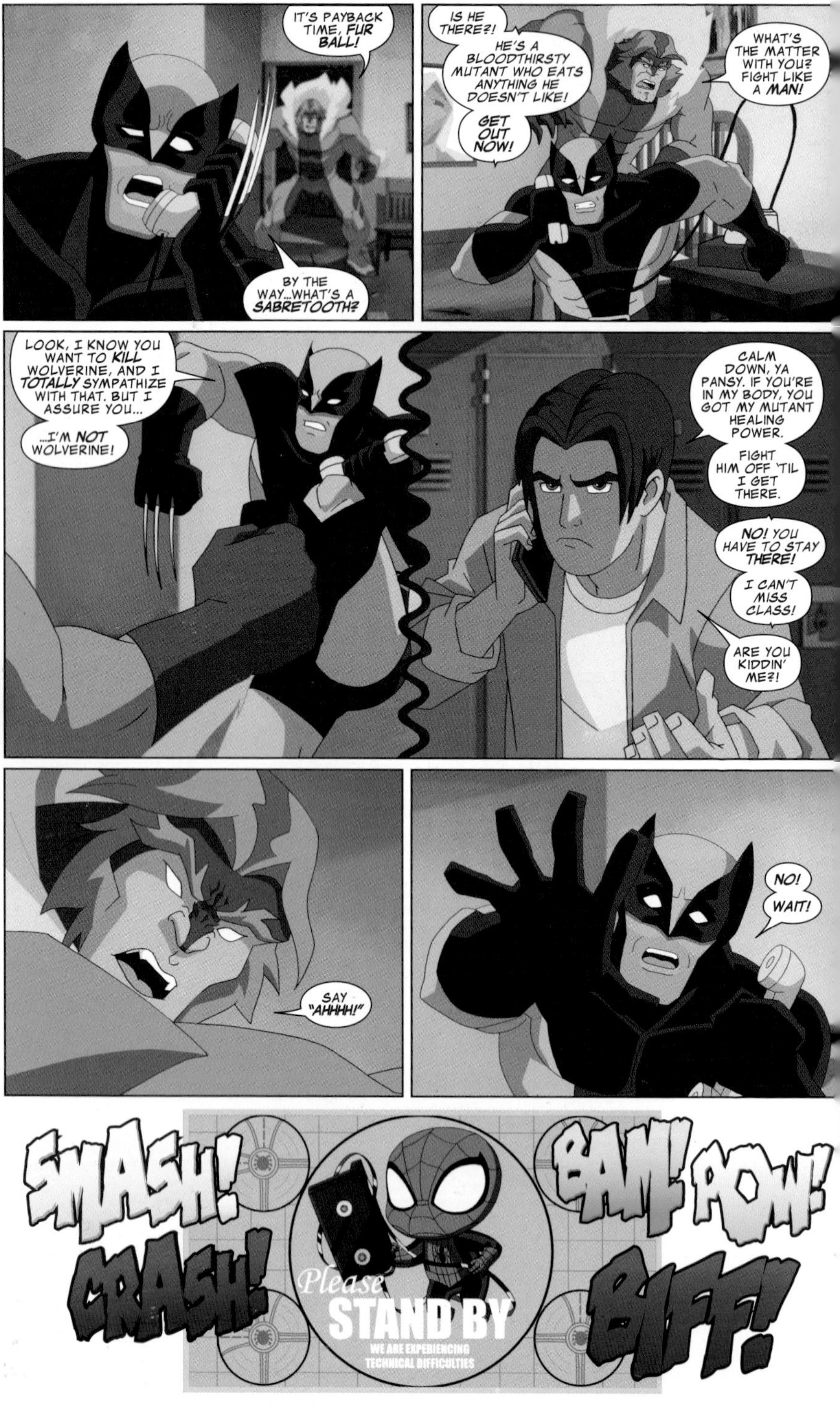

IT'S PAYBACK TIME, FUR BALL!
BY THE WAY...WHAT'S A SABRETOOTH?
IS HE THERE?!
HE'S A BLOODTHIRSTY MUTANT WHO EATS ANYTHING HE DOESN'T LIKE!
GET OUT NOW!
WHAT'S THE MATTER WITH YOU? FIGHT LIKE A MAN!
LOOK, I KNOW YOU WANT TO KILL WOLVERINE, AND I TOTALLY SYMPATHIZE WITH THAT. BUT I ASSURE YOU...
...I'M NOT WOLVERINE!
CALM DOWN, YA PANSY. IF YOU'RE IN MY BODY, YOU GOT MY MUTANT HEALING POWER.
FIGHT HIM OFF 'TIL I GET THERE.
NO! YOU HAVE TO STAY THERE!
I CAN'T MISS CLASS!
ARE YOU KIDDIN' ME?!
SAY "AHHHH!"
NO!
WAIT!
SMASH!
CRASH!
Please STAND BY
WE ARE EXPERIENCING TECHNICAL DIFFICULTIES
BAM!
POW!
BIFF!

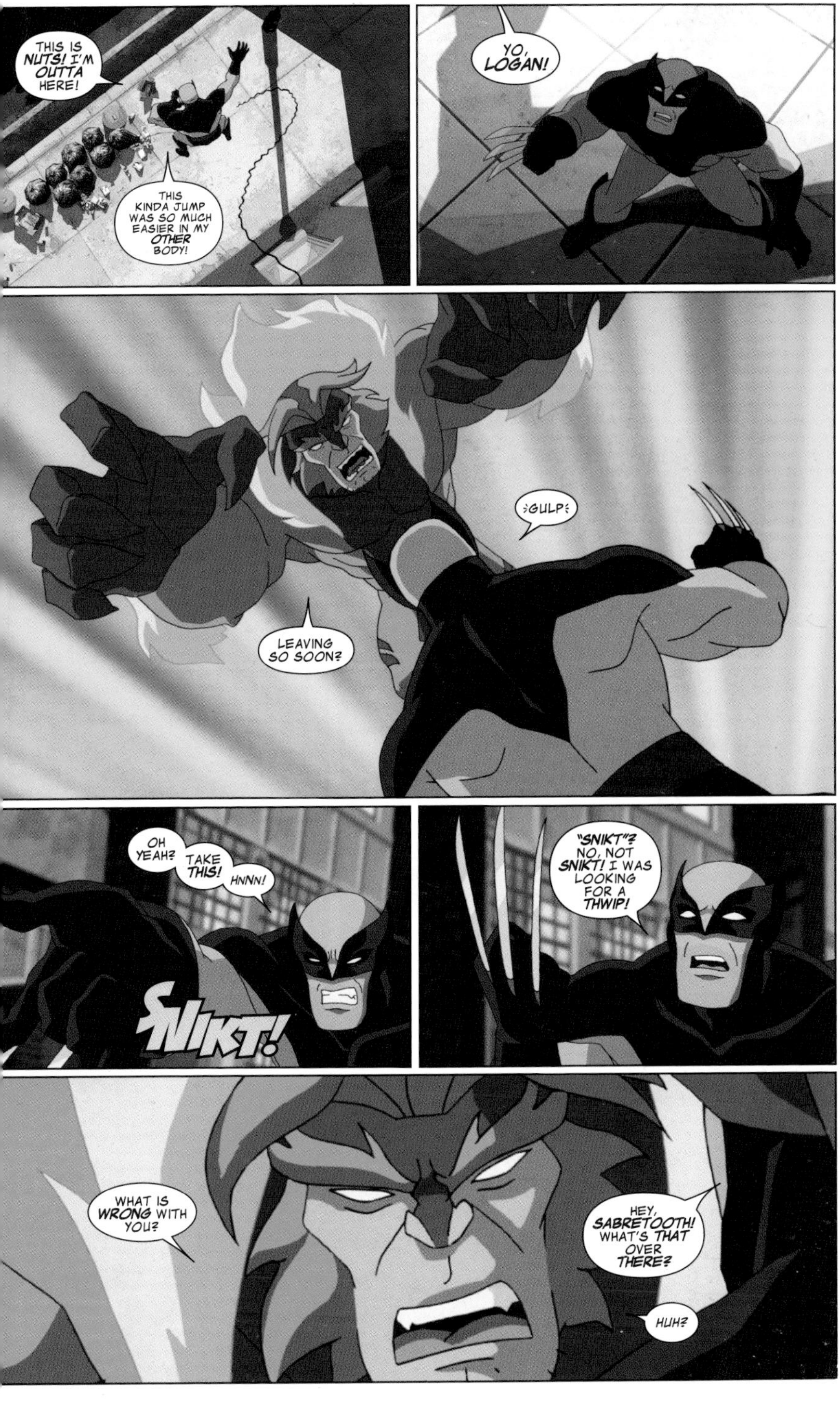
THIS IS NUTS! I'M OUTTA HERE!
THIS KINDA JUMP WAS SO MUCH EASIER IN MY OTHER BODY!
YO, LOGAN!
LEAVING SO SOON?
GULP
OH YEAH?
TAKE THIS!
HNNN!
SNIKT!
"SNIKT"? NO, NOT SNIKT! I WAS LOOKING FOR A THWIP!
WHAT IS WRONG WITH YOU?
HEY, SABRETOOTH! WHAT'S THAT OVER THERE?
HUH?

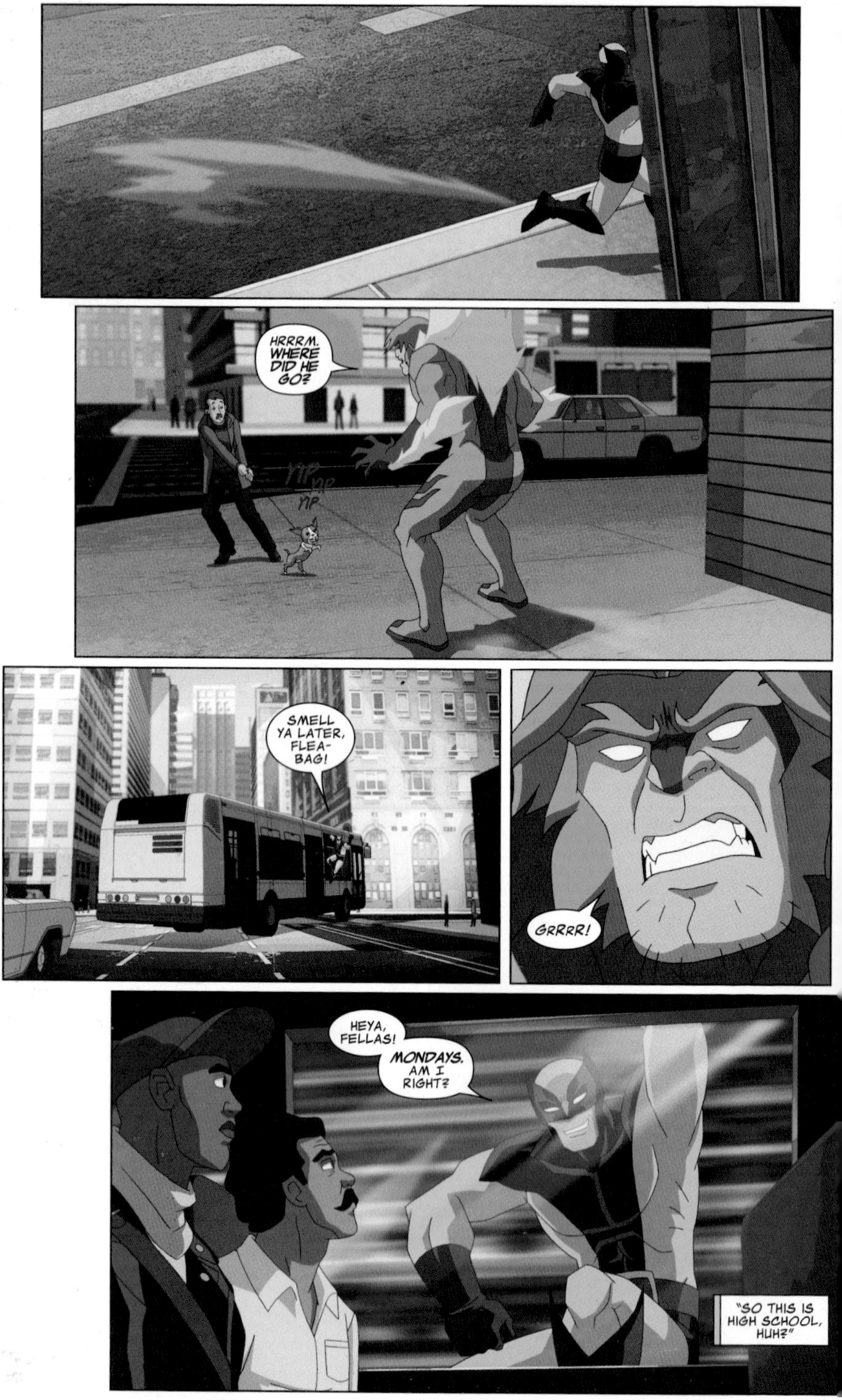
HRRRM. WHERE DID HE GO?
YIP YIP YIP
SMELL YA LATER, FLEA-BAG!
GRRRR!
HEYA, FELLAS!
MONDAYS. AM I RIGHT?
"SO THIS IS HIGH SCHOOL, HUH?"

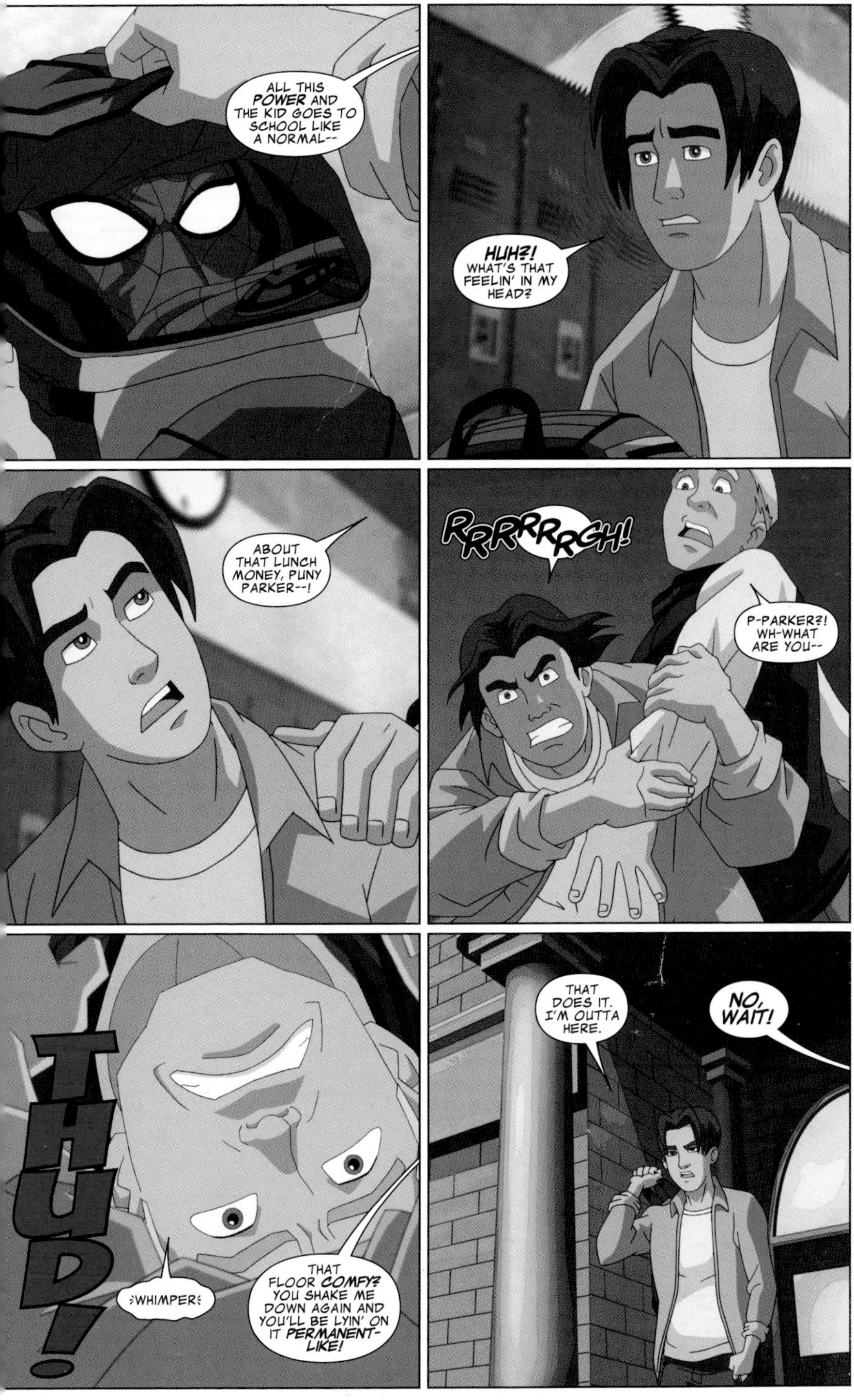
ALL THIS POWER AND THE KID GOES TO SCHOOL LIKE A NORMAL--
HUH?! WHAT'S THAT FEELIN' IN MY HEAD?
ABOUT THAT LUNCH MONEY, PUNY PARKER--!
RRRRRRRGH!
P-PARKER?! WH-WHAT ARE YOU--
THUD!
WHIMPER
THAT FLOOR COMFY? YOU SHAKE ME DOWN AGAIN AND YOU'LL BE LYIN' ON IT PERMANENT-LIKE!
THAT DOES IT. I'M OUTTA HERE.
NO, WAIT!

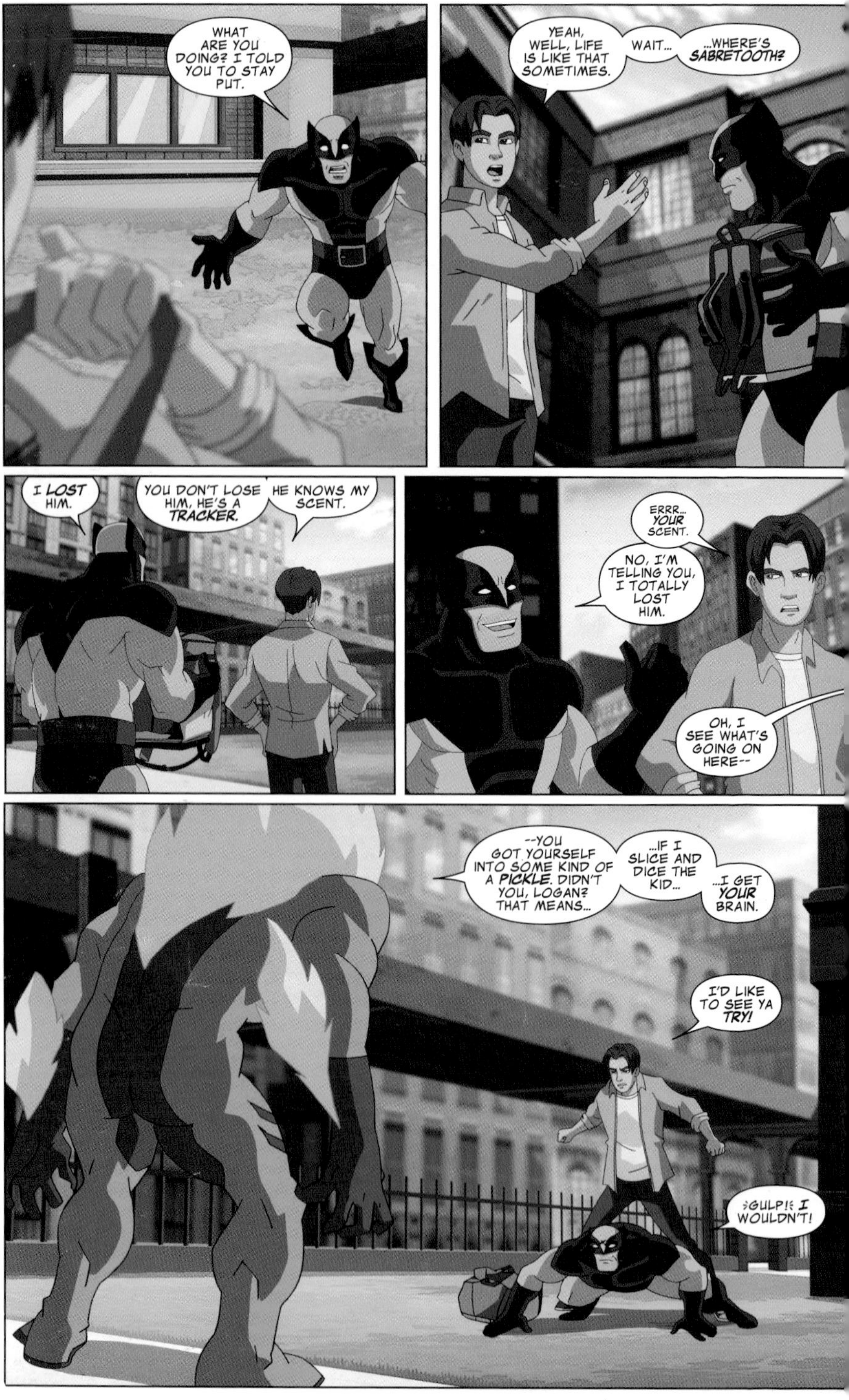
WHAT ARE YOU DOING? I TOLD YOU TO STAY PUT.
YEAH, WELL, LIFE IS LIKE THAT SOMETIMES.
WAIT...
...WHERE'S SABRETOOTH?
I LOST HIM.
YOU DON'T LOSE HIM, HE'S A TRACKER.
HE KNOWS MY SCENT.
ERRR... YOUR SCENT.
NO, I'M TELLING YOU, I TOTALLY LOST HIM.
OH, I SEE WHAT'S GOING ON HERE--
--YOU GOT YOURSELF INTO SOME KIND OF A PICKLE. DIDN'T YOU, LOGAN? THAT MEANS...
...IF I SLICE AND DICE THE KID...
...I GET YOUR BRAIN.
I'D LIKE TO SEE YA TRY!
GULP! I WOULDN'T!

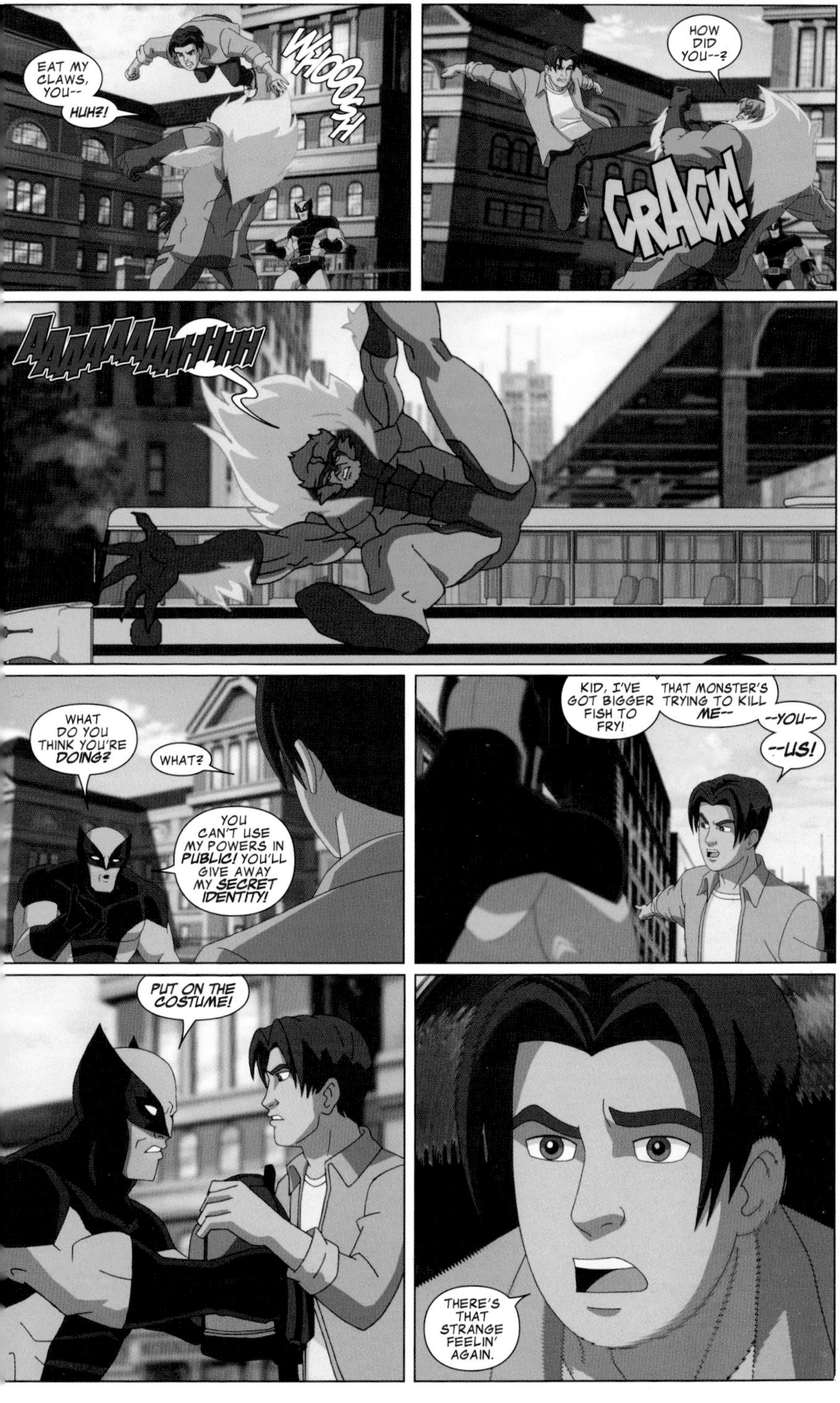
EAT MY CLAWS, YOU--
HUH?!
WHOOOSH
HOW DID YOU--?
CRACK!
AAAAAAAAHHHH
WHAT DO YOU THINK YOU'RE DOING?
WHAT?
YOU CAN'T USE MY POWERS IN PUBLIC! YOU'LL GIVE AWAY MY SECRET IDENTITY!
KID, I'VE GOT BIGGER FISH TO FRY!
THAT MONSTER'S TRYING TO KILL ME--
--YOU--
--US!
PUT ON THE COSTUME!
THERE'S THAT STRANGE FEELIN' AGAIN.

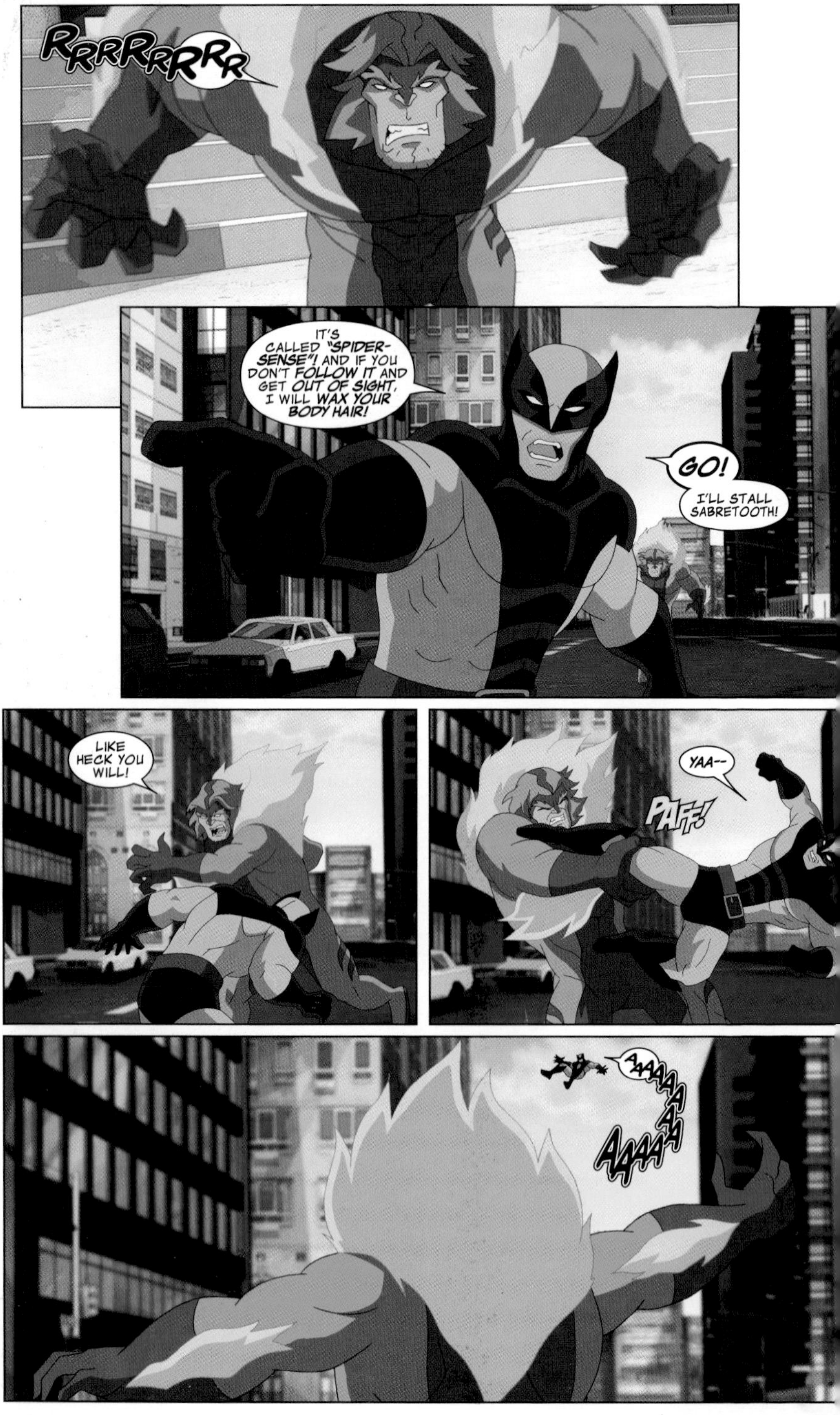
RRRRRRRR
IT'S CALLED "SPIDER-SENSE"! AND IF YOU DON'T FOLLOW IT AND GET OUT OF SIGHT, I WILL WAX YOUR BODY HAIR!
GO!
I'LL STALL SABRETOOTH!
LIKE HECK YOU WILL!
YAA--
PAFF!
AAAAAAAAAAAA

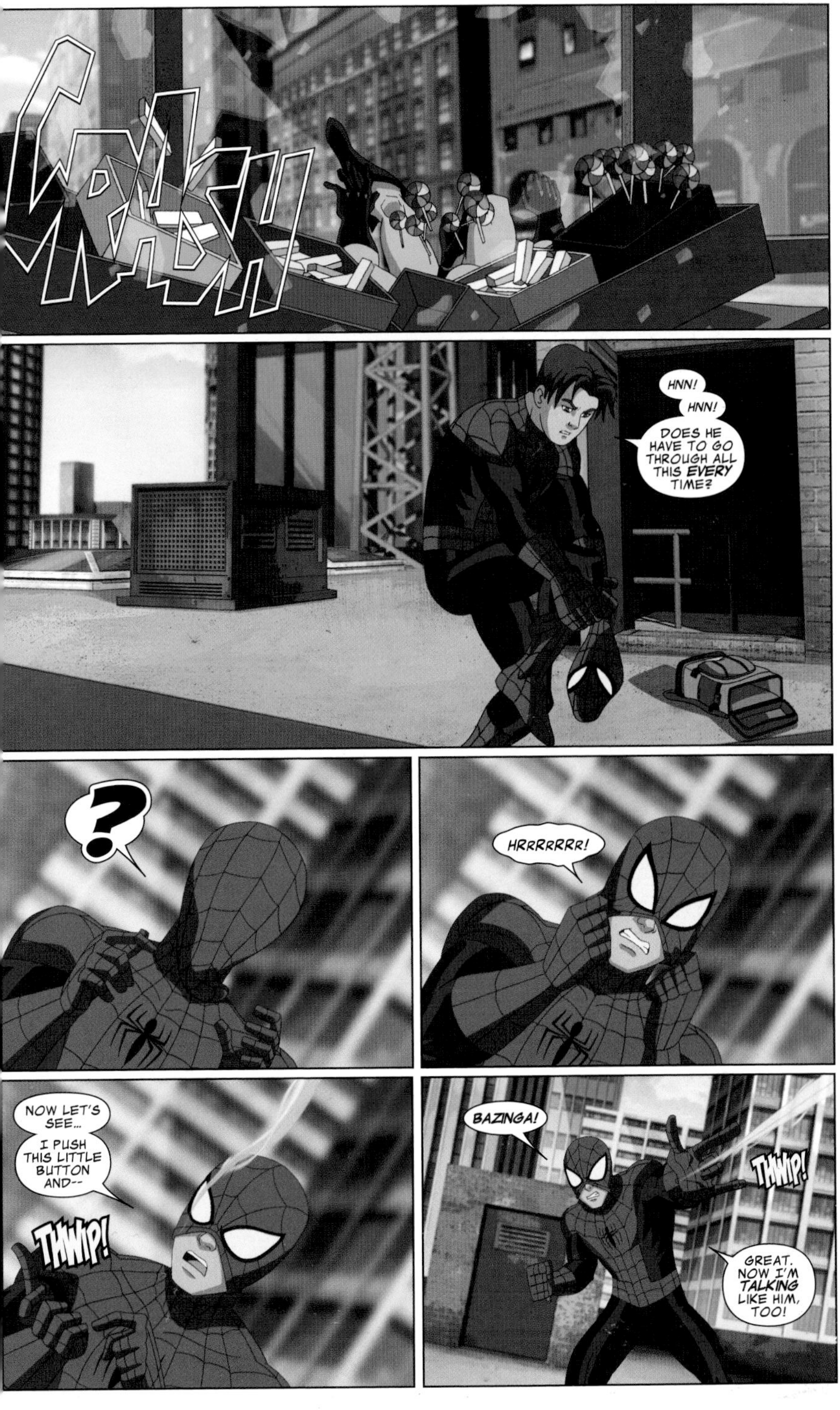
HNN!
HNN!
DOES HE HAVE TO GO THROUGH ALL THIS *EVERY* TIME?
?
HRRRRRRR!
NOW LET'S SEE... I PUSH THIS LITTLE BUTTON AND--
THWIP!
BAZINGA!
THWIP!
GREAT. NOW I'M *TALKING* LIKE HIM, TOO!

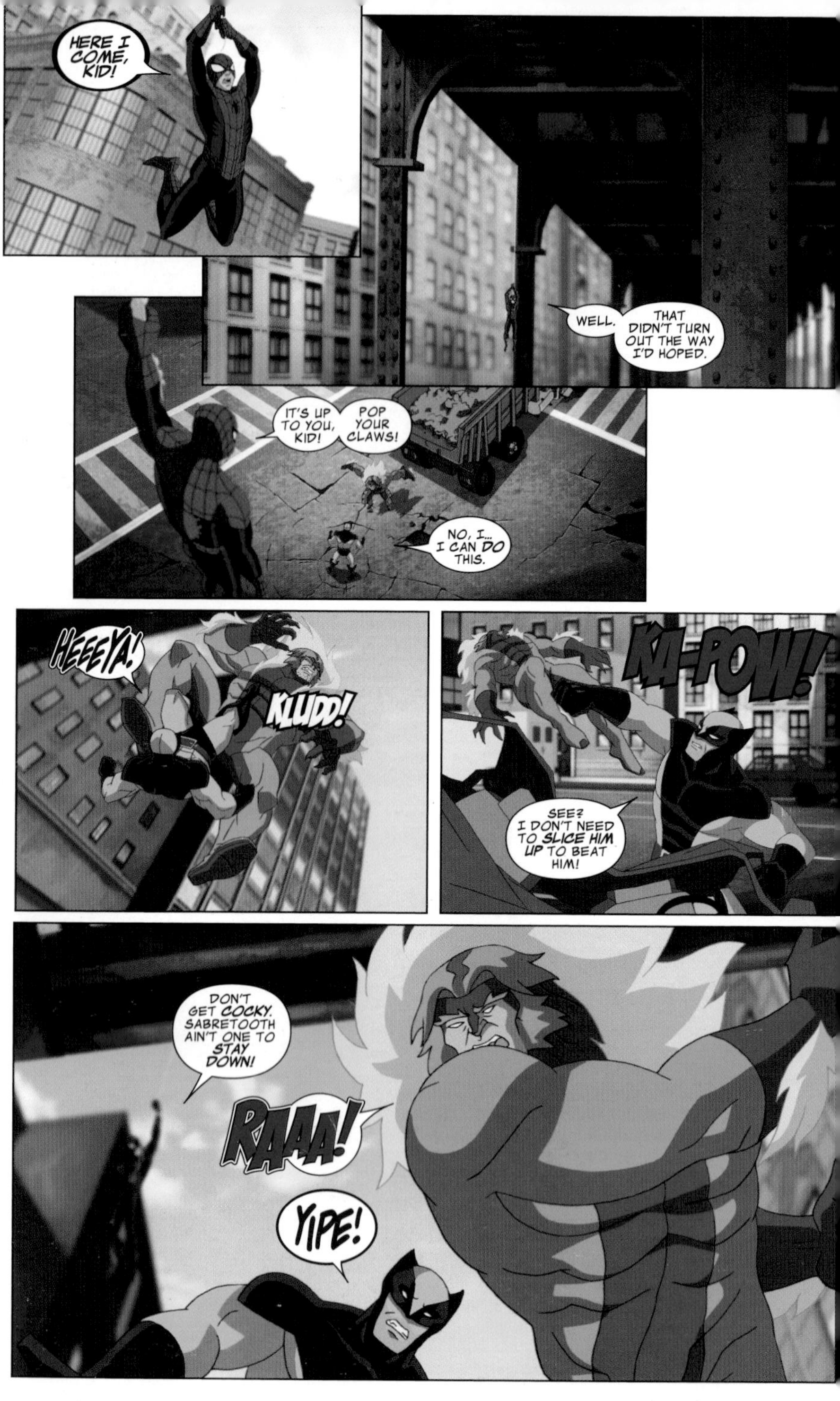
HERE I COME, KID!
WELL.
THAT DIDN'T TURN OUT THE WAY I'D HOPED.
IT'S UP TO YOU, KID!
POP YOUR CLAWS!
NO, I... I CAN DO THIS.
HEEEYA!
KLUDD!
KA-POW!
SEE? I DON'T NEED TO SLICE HIM UP TO BEAT HIM!
DON'T GET COCKY. SABRETOOTH AIN'T ONE TO STAY DOWN!
RAAA!
YIPE!

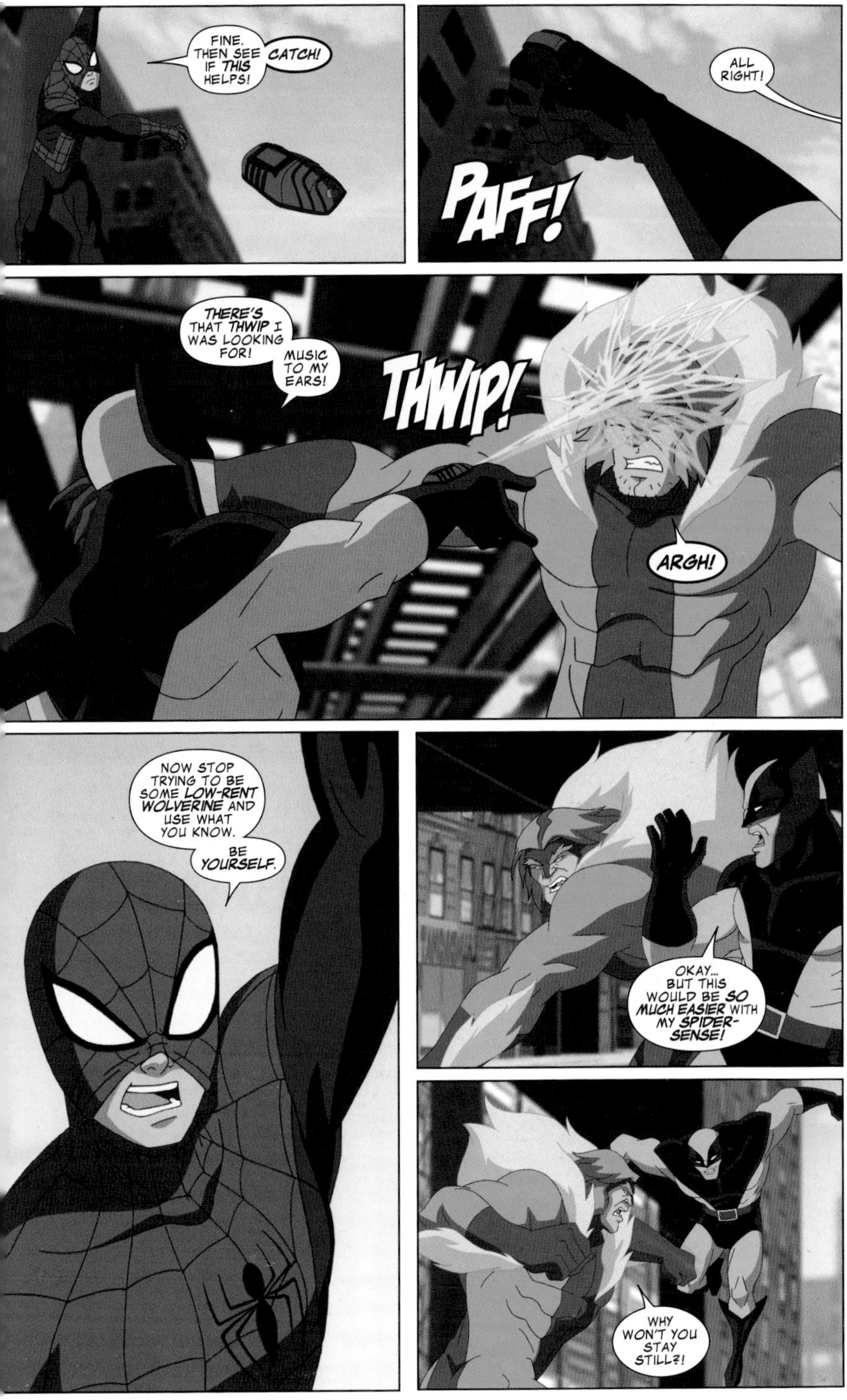
FINE. THEN SEE IF THIS HELPS!
CATCH!
ALL RIGHT!
PAFF!
THERE'S THAT THWIP I WAS LOOKING FOR!
MUSIC TO MY EARS!
THWIP!
ARGH!
NOW STOP TRYING TO BE SOME LOW-RENT WOLVERINE AND USE WHAT YOU KNOW.
BE YOURSELF.
OKAY... BUT THIS WOULD BE SO MUCH EASIER WITH MY SPIDER-SENSE!
WHY WON'T YOU STAY STILL?!

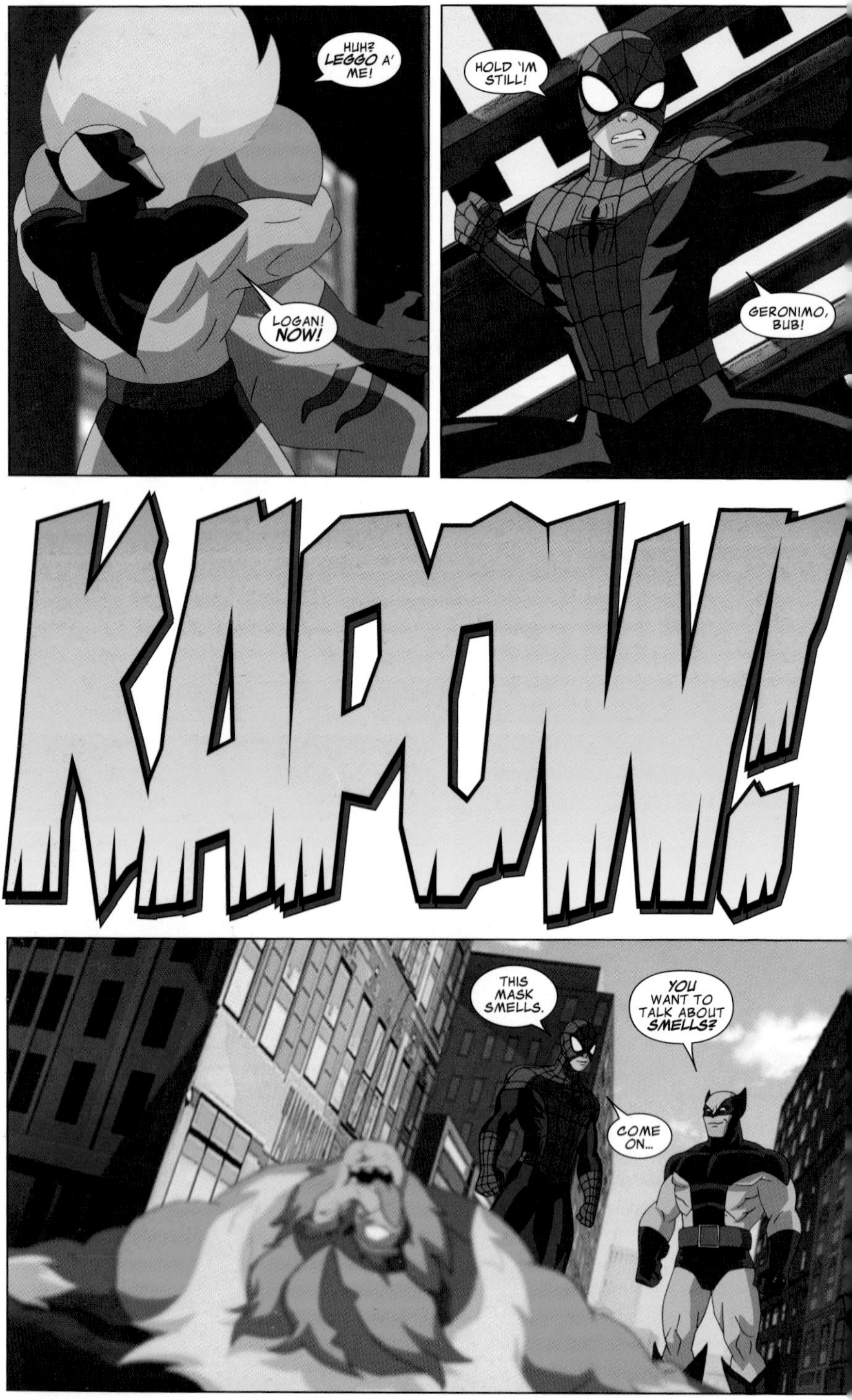
HUH? LEGGO A' ME!
LOGAN! NOW!
HOLD 'IM STILL!
GERONIMO, BUB!
KAPOW!
THIS MASK SMELLS.
YOU WANT TO TALK ABOUT SMELLS?
COME ON...

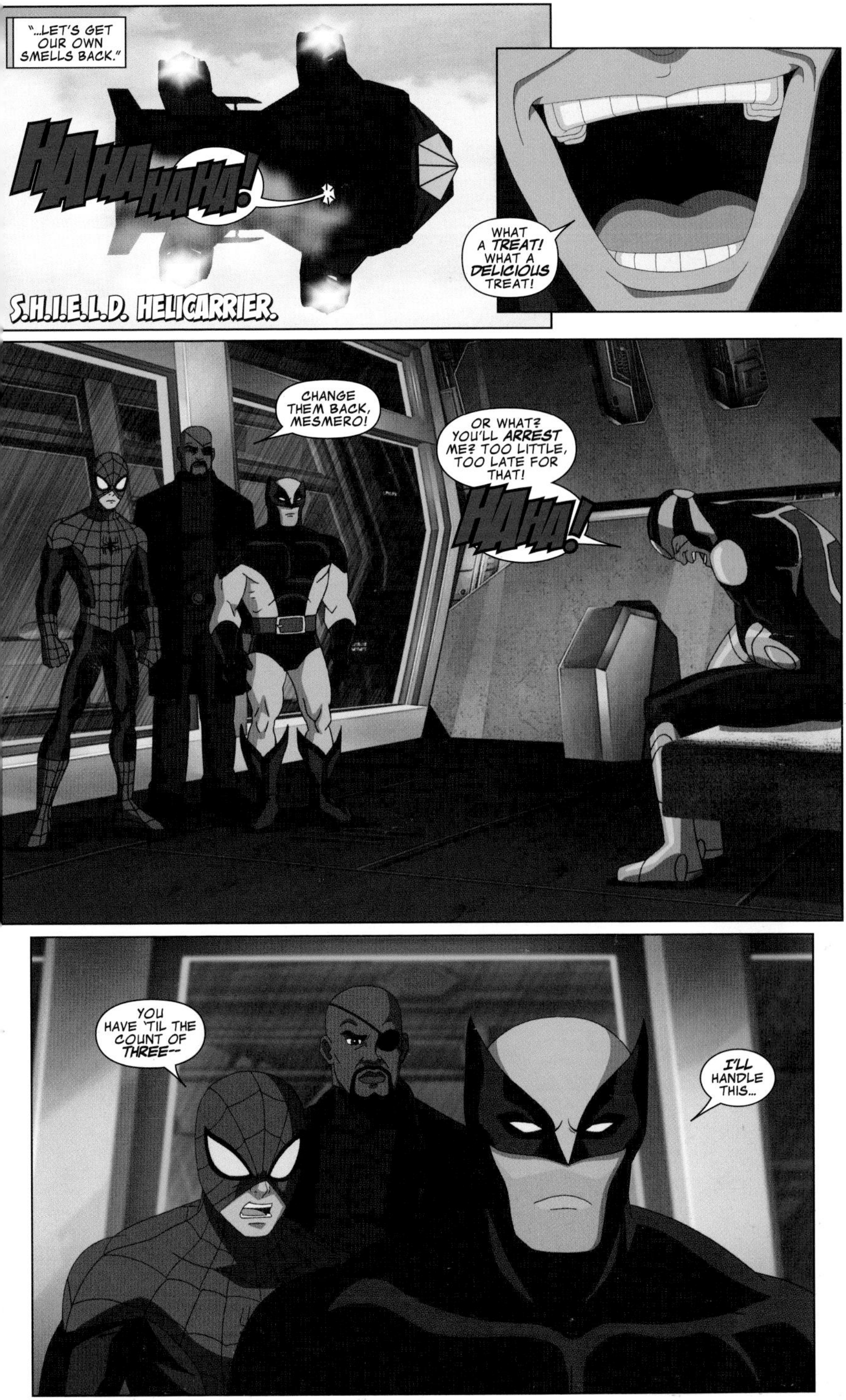
"...LET'S GET OUR OWN SMELLS BACK."
HAHAHAHA!
S.H.I.E.L.D. HELICARRIER.
WHAT A TREAT! WHAT A DELICIOUS TREAT!
CHANGE THEM BACK, MESMERO!
OR WHAT? YOU'LL ARREST ME? TOO LITTLE, TOO LATE FOR THAT!
HAHA!
YOU HAVE 'TIL THE COUNT OF THREE--
I'LL HANDLE THIS...

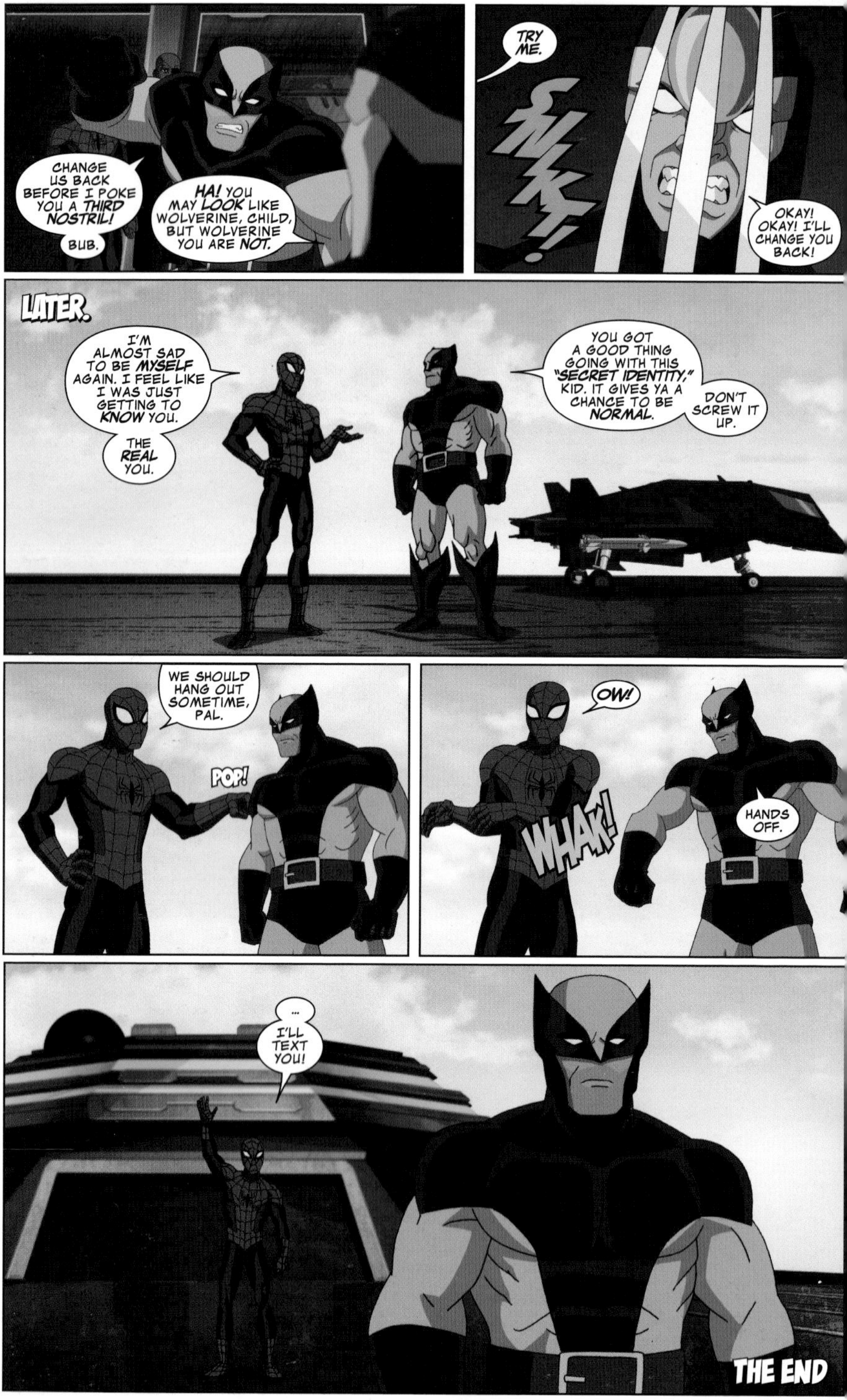
CHANGE US BACK BEFORE I POKE YOU A THIRD NOSTRIL!
BUB.
HA! YOU MAY LOOK LIKE WOLVERINE, CHILD, BUT WOLVERINE YOU ARE NOT.
TRY ME.
SNIKT!
OKAY! OKAY! I'LL CHANGE YOU BACK!
LATER.
I'M ALMOST SAD TO BE MYSELF AGAIN. I FEEL LIKE I WAS JUST GETTING TO KNOW YOU.
THE REAL YOU.
YOU GOT A GOOD THING GOING WITH THIS "SECRET IDENTITY," KID. IT GIVES YA A CHANCE TO BE NORMAL.
DON'T SCREW IT UP.
WE SHOULD HANG OUT SOMETIME, PAL.
POP!
OW!
WHAK!
HANDS OFF.
...
I'LL TEXT YOU!
THE END

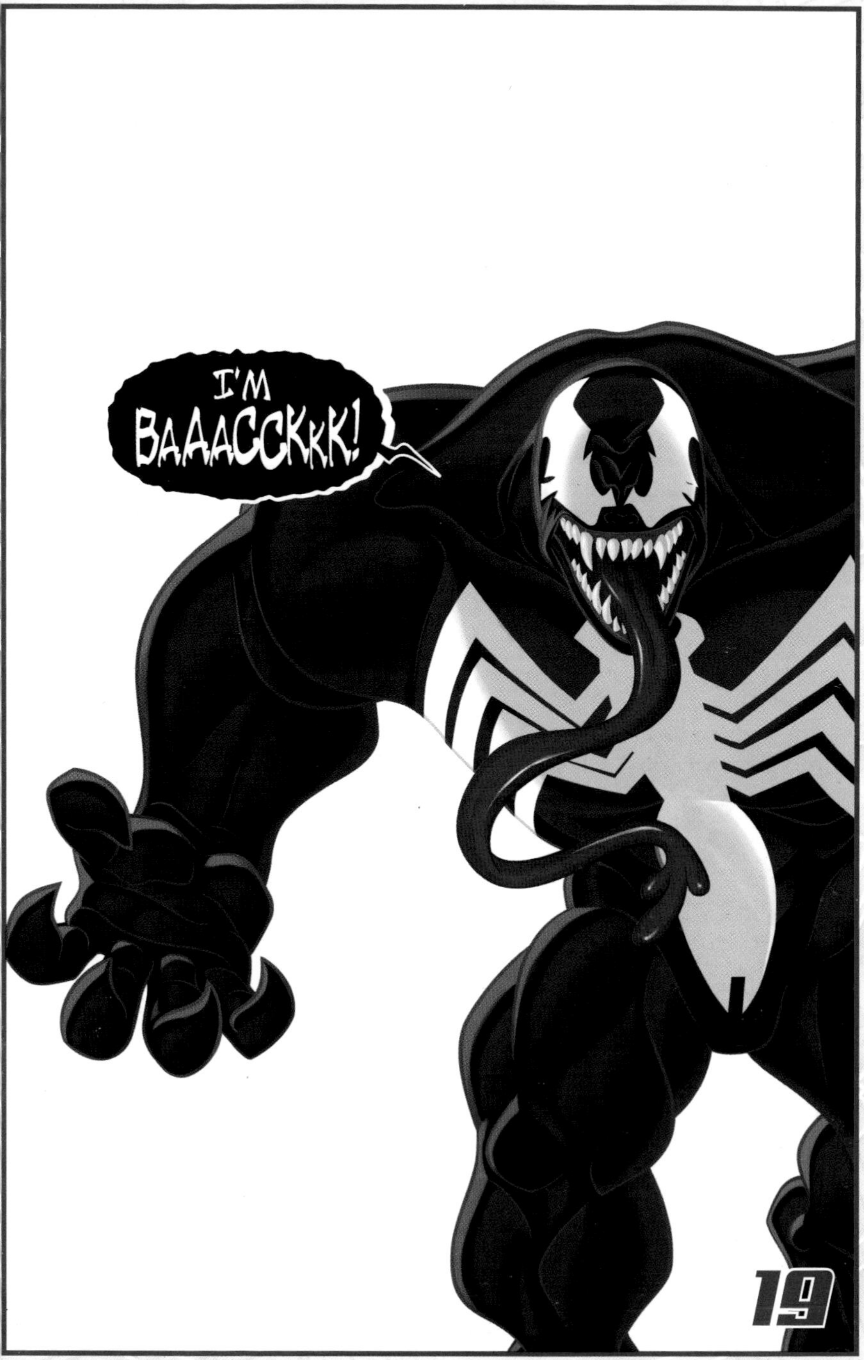
I'M BAAACCKKK!

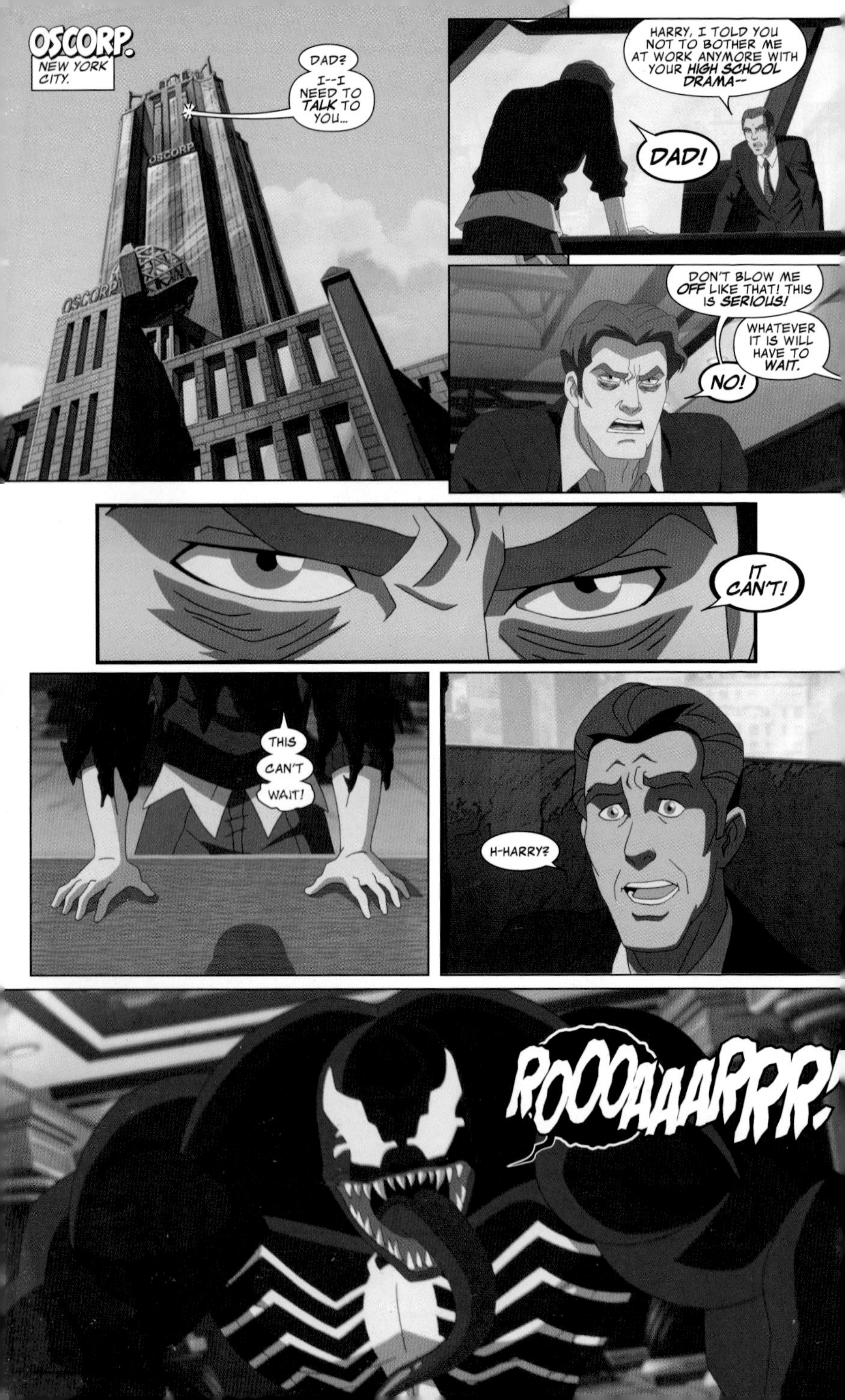
OSCORP.
NEW YORK CITY.
DAD? I--I NEED TO TALK TO YOU...
HARRY, I TOLD YOU NOT TO BOTHER ME AT WORK ANYMORE WITH YOUR HIGH SCHOOL DRAMA--
DAD!
DON'T BLOW ME OFF LIKE THAT! THIS IS SERIOUS!
WHATEVER IT IS WILL HAVE TO WAIT.
NO!
IT CAN'T!
THIS CAN'T WAIT!
H-HARRY?
ROOOAAAARRRR!

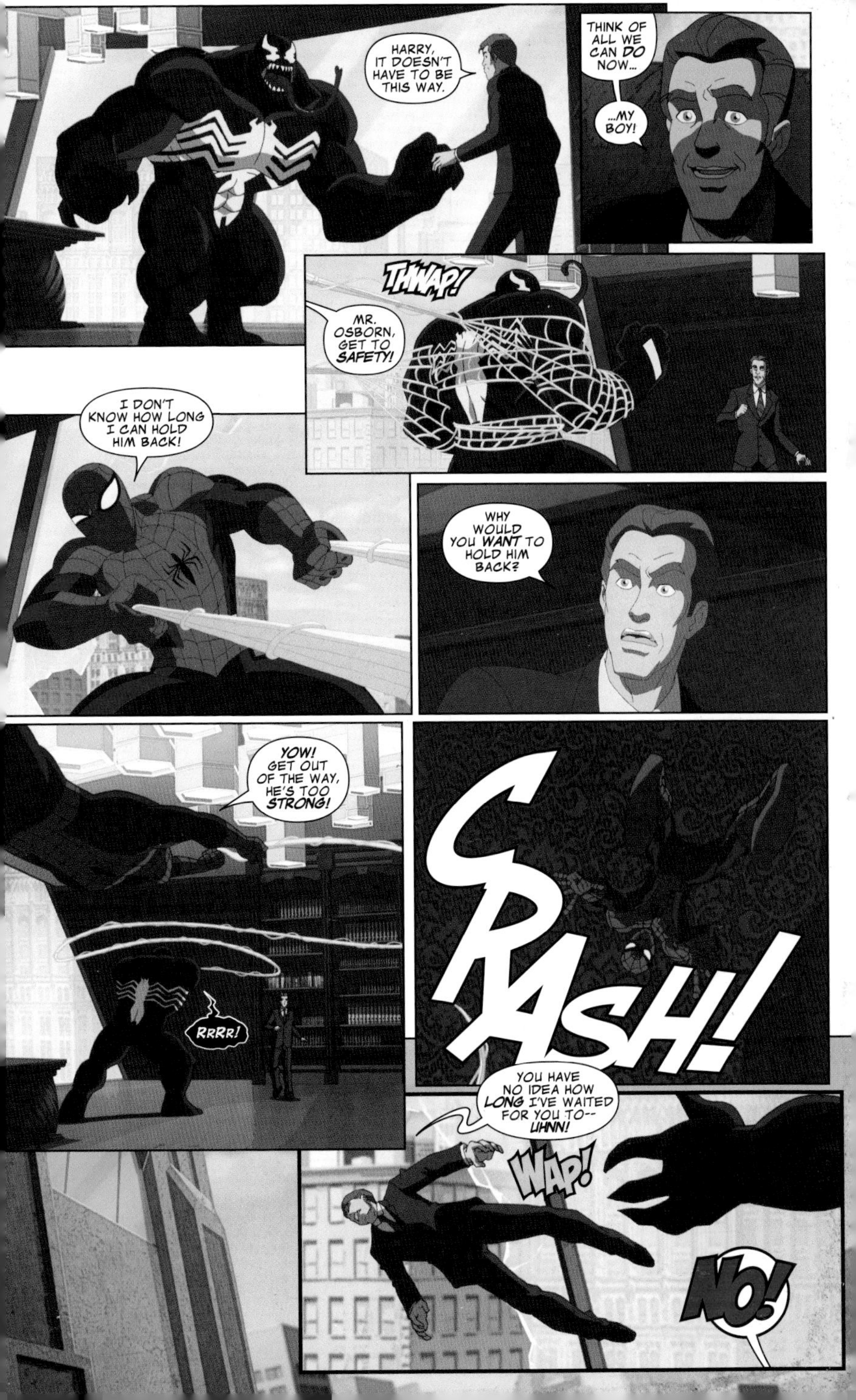
HARRY, IT DOESN'T HAVE TO BE THIS WAY.
THINK OF ALL WE CAN DO NOW...
...MY BOY!
THWAP!
MR. OSBORN, GET TO SAFETY!
I DON'T KNOW HOW LONG I CAN HOLD HIM BACK!
WHY WOULD YOU WANT TO HOLD HIM BACK?
YOW! GET OUT OF THE WAY, HE'S TOO STRONG!
RRRR!
CRASH!
YOU HAVE NO IDEA HOW LONG I'VE WAITED FOR YOU TO-- UHNN!
WAP!
NO!

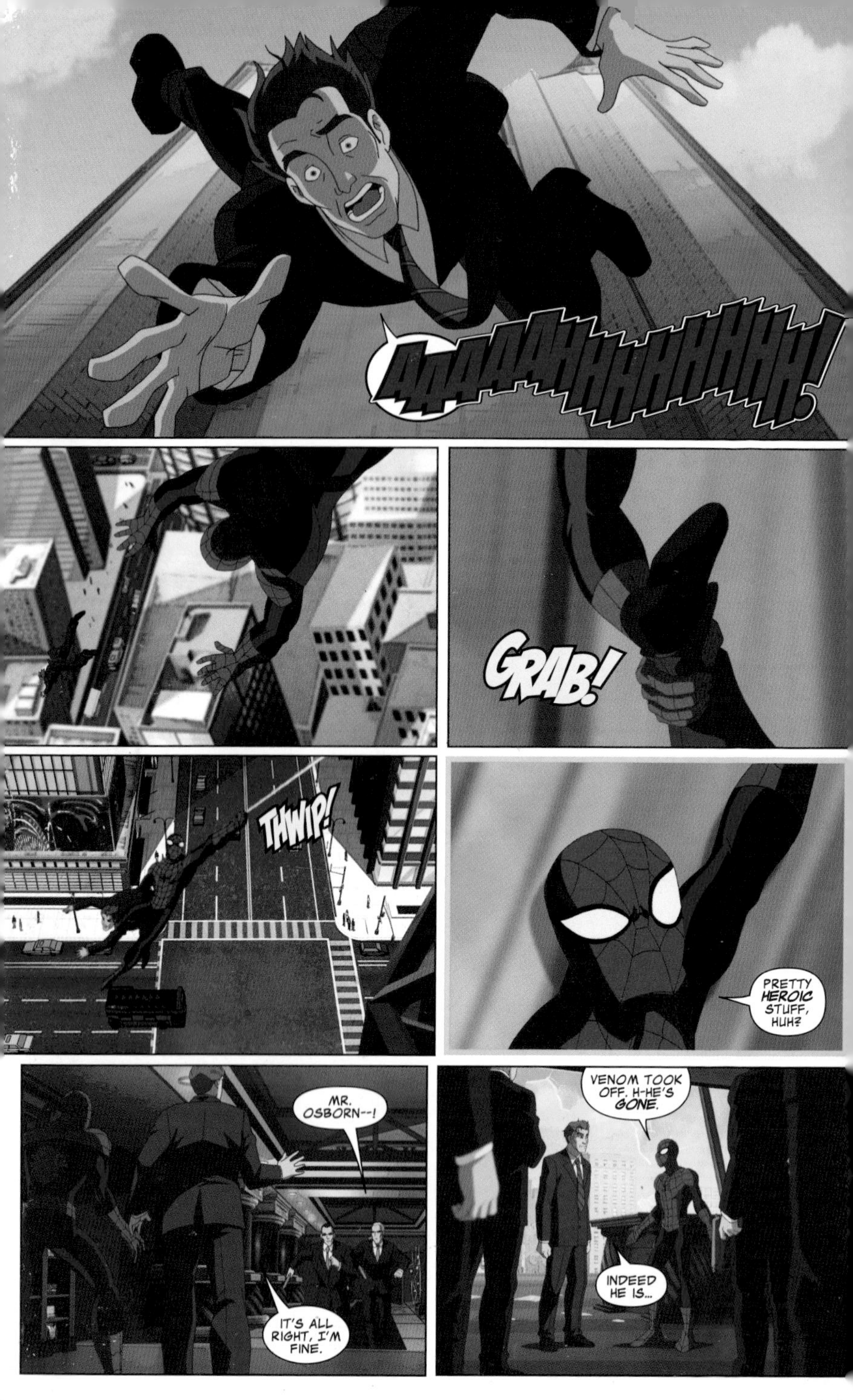
AAAAAHHHHHHHHH!
GRAB!
THWIP!
PRETTY HEROIC STUFF, HUH?
MR. OSBORN--!
IT'S ALL RIGHT, I'M FINE.
VENOM TOOK OFF. H-HE'S GONE.
INDEED HE IS...

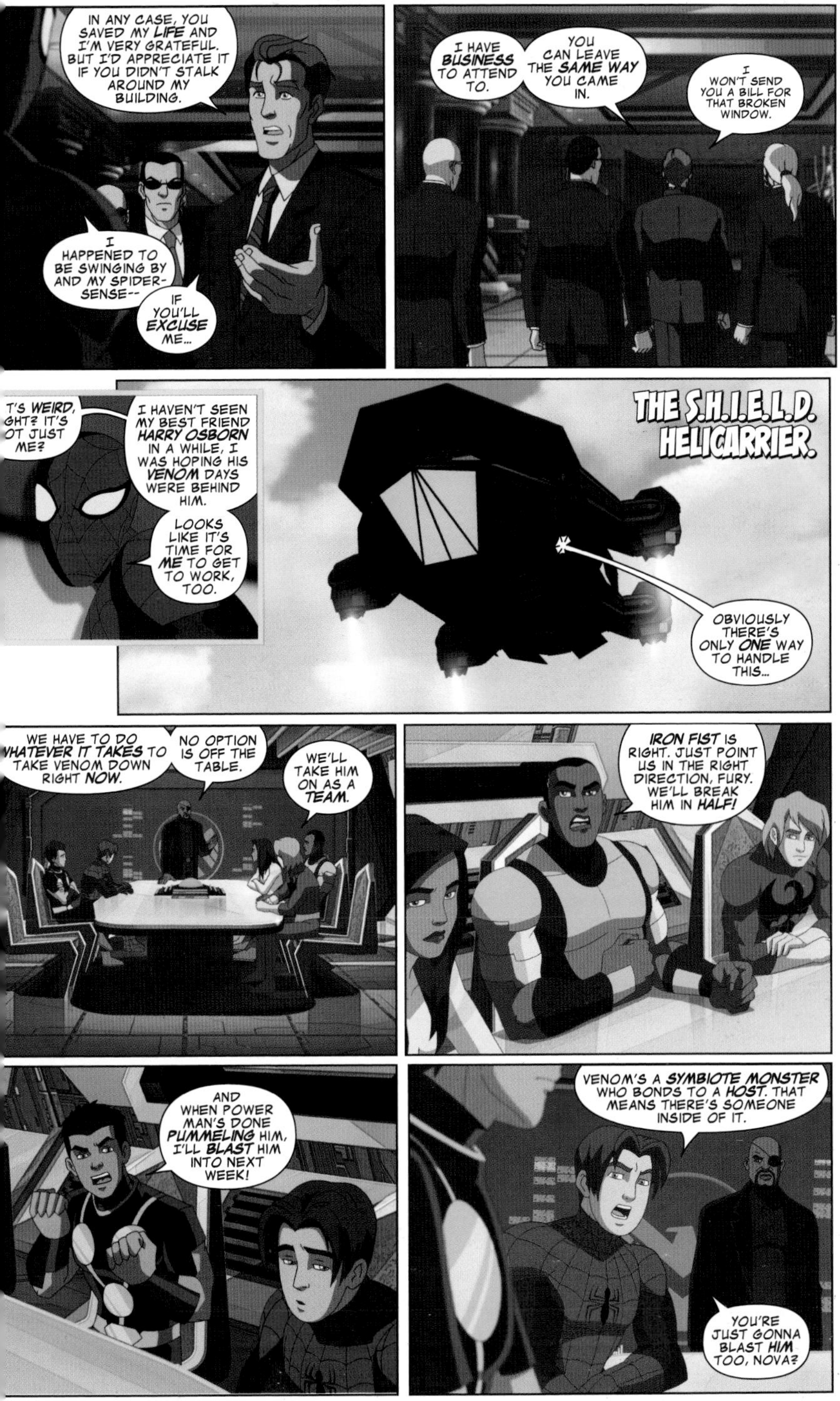

IN ANY CASE, YOU SAVED MY LIFE AND I'M VERY GRATEFUL. BUT I'D APPRECIATE IT IF YOU DIDN'T STALK AROUND MY BUILDING.
I HAPPENED TO BE SWINGING BY AND MY SPIDER-SENSE--
IF YOU'LL EXCUSE ME...
I HAVE BUSINESS TO ATTEND TO.
YOU CAN LEAVE THE SAME WAY YOU CAME IN.
I WON'T SEND YOU A BILL FOR THAT BROKEN WINDOW.
THE S.H.I.E.L.D. HELICARRIER.
T'S WEIRD, GHT? IT'S OT JUST ME?
I HAVEN'T SEEN MY BEST FRIEND HARRY OSBORN IN A WHILE, I WAS HOPING HIS VENOM DAYS WERE BEHIND HIM.
LOOKS LIKE IT'S TIME FOR ME TO GET TO WORK, TOO.
OBVIOUSLY THERE'S ONLY ONE WAY TO HANDLE THIS...
WE HAVE TO DO WHATEVER IT TAKES TO TAKE VENOM DOWN RIGHT NOW.
NO OPTION IS OFF THE TABLE.
WE'LL TAKE HIM ON AS A TEAM.
IRON FIST IS RIGHT. JUST POINT US IN THE RIGHT DIRECTION, FURY. WE'LL BREAK HIM IN HALF!
AND WHEN POWER MAN'S DONE PUMMELING HIM, I'LL BLAST HIM INTO NEXT WEEK!
VENOM'S A SYMBIOTE MONSTER WHO BONDS TO A HOST. THAT MEANS THERE'S SOMEONE INSIDE OF IT.
YOU'RE JUST GONNA BLAST HIM TOO, NOVA?

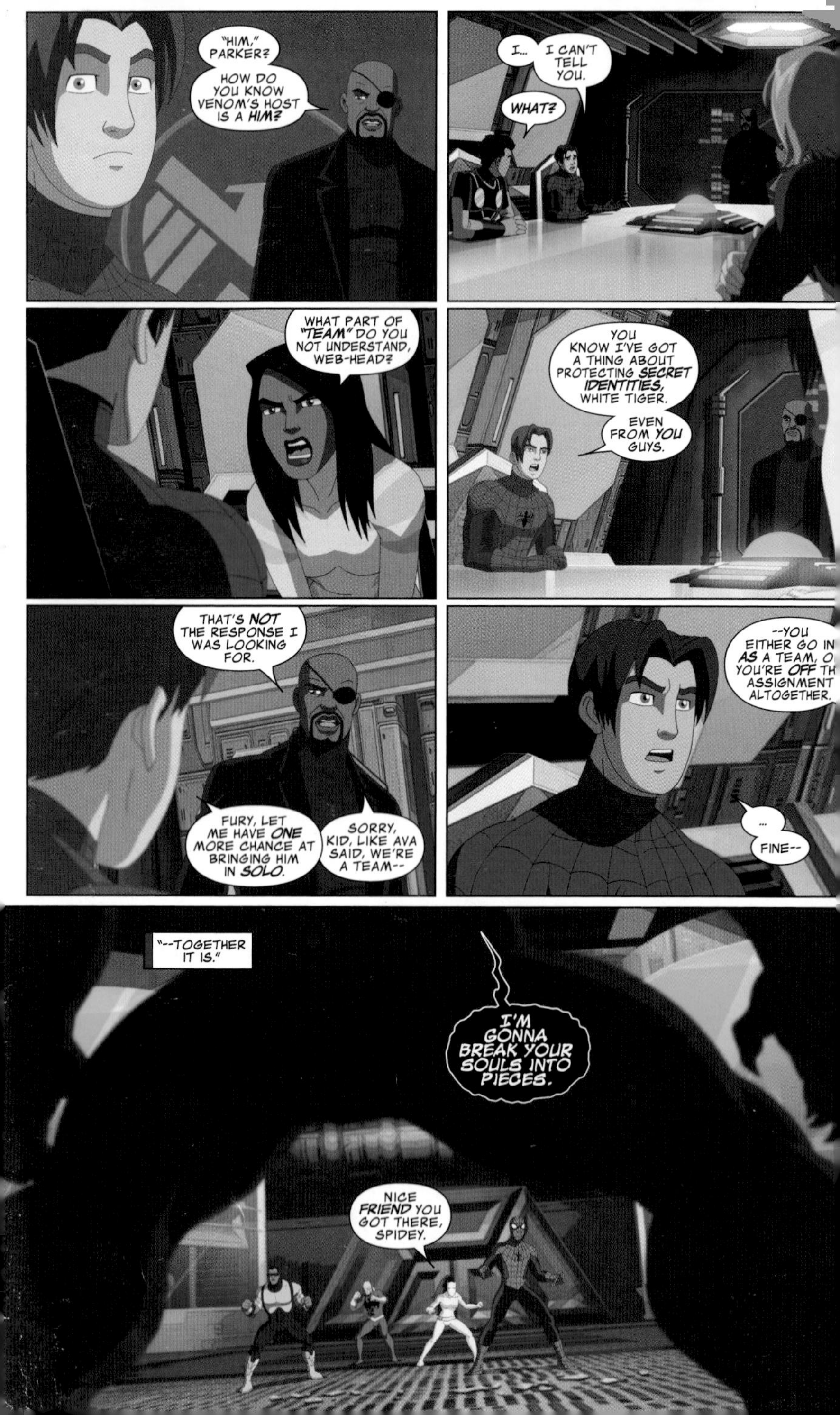
"HIM," PARKER?
HOW DO YOU KNOW VENOM'S HOST IS A HIM?
I... I CAN'T TELL YOU.
WHAT?
WHAT PART OF "TEAM" DO YOU NOT UNDERSTAND, WEB-HEAD?
YOU KNOW I'VE GOT A THING ABOUT PROTECTING SECRET IDENTITIES, WHITE TIGER.
EVEN FROM YOU GUYS.
THAT'S NOT THE RESPONSE I WAS LOOKING FOR.
FURY, LET ME HAVE ONE MORE CHANCE AT BRINGING HIM IN SOLO.
SORRY, KID, LIKE AVA SAID, WE'RE A TEAM--
--YOU EITHER GO IN AS A TEAM, O YOU'RE OFF TH ASSIGNMENT ALTOGETHER.
... FINE--
"--TOGETHER IT IS."
I'M GONNA BREAK YOUR SOULS INTO PIECES.
NICE FRIEND YOU GOT THERE, SPIDEY.

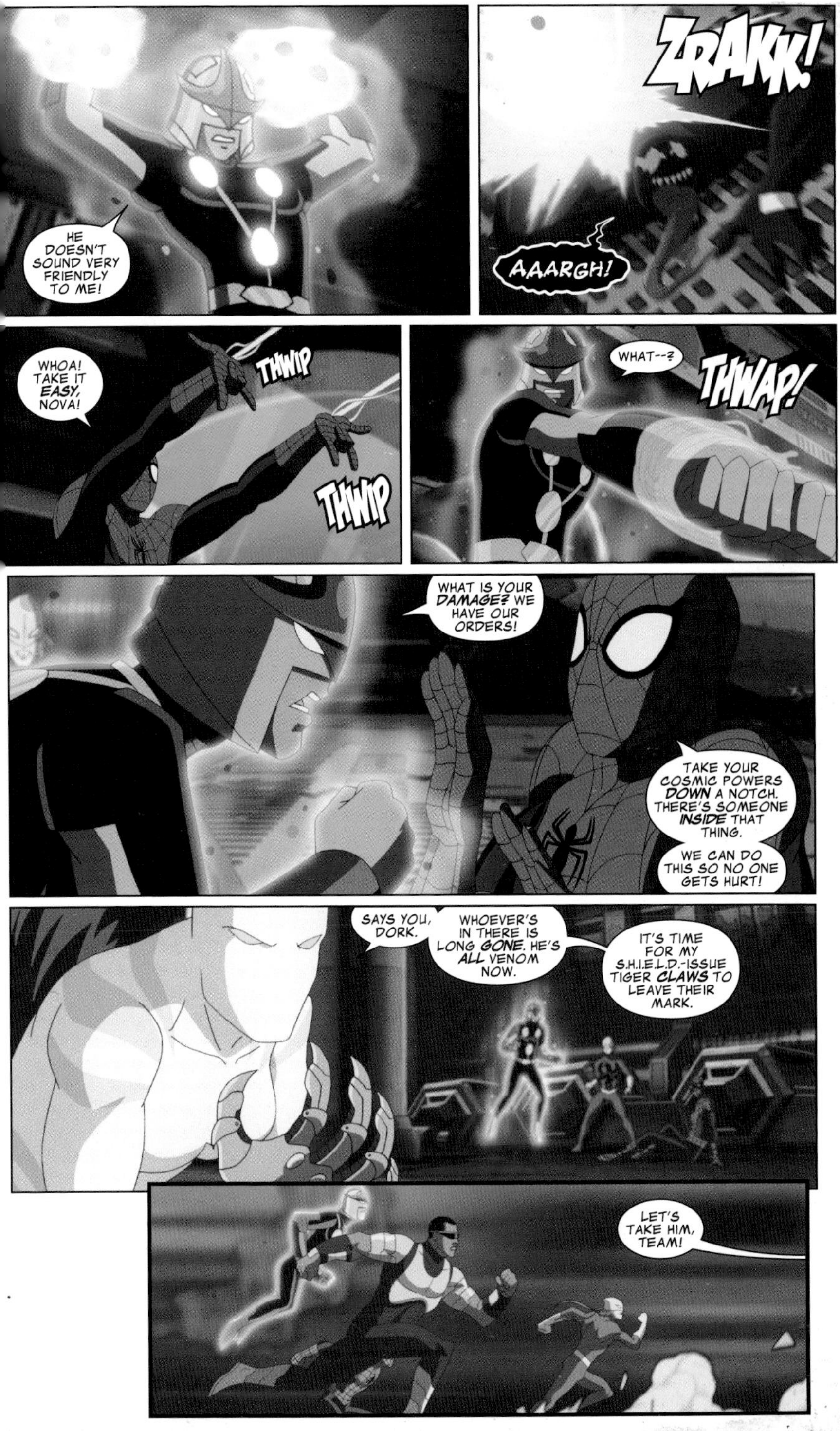

HE DOESN'T SOUND VERY FRIENDLY TO ME!
ZRAKK!
AAARGH!
WHOA! TAKE IT EASY, NOVA!
THWIP
THWIP
WHAT--?
THWAP!
WHAT IS YOUR DAMAGE? WE HAVE OUR ORDERS!
TAKE YOUR COSMIC POWERS DOWN A NOTCH. THERE'S SOMEONE INSIDE THAT THING.
WE CAN DO THIS SO NO ONE GETS HURT!
SAYS YOU, DORK.
WHOEVER'S IN THERE IS LONG GONE. HE'S ALL VENOM NOW.
IT'S TIME FOR MY S.H.I.E.L.D.-ISSUE TIGER CLAWS TO LEAVE THEIR MARK.
LET'S TAKE HIM, TEAM!

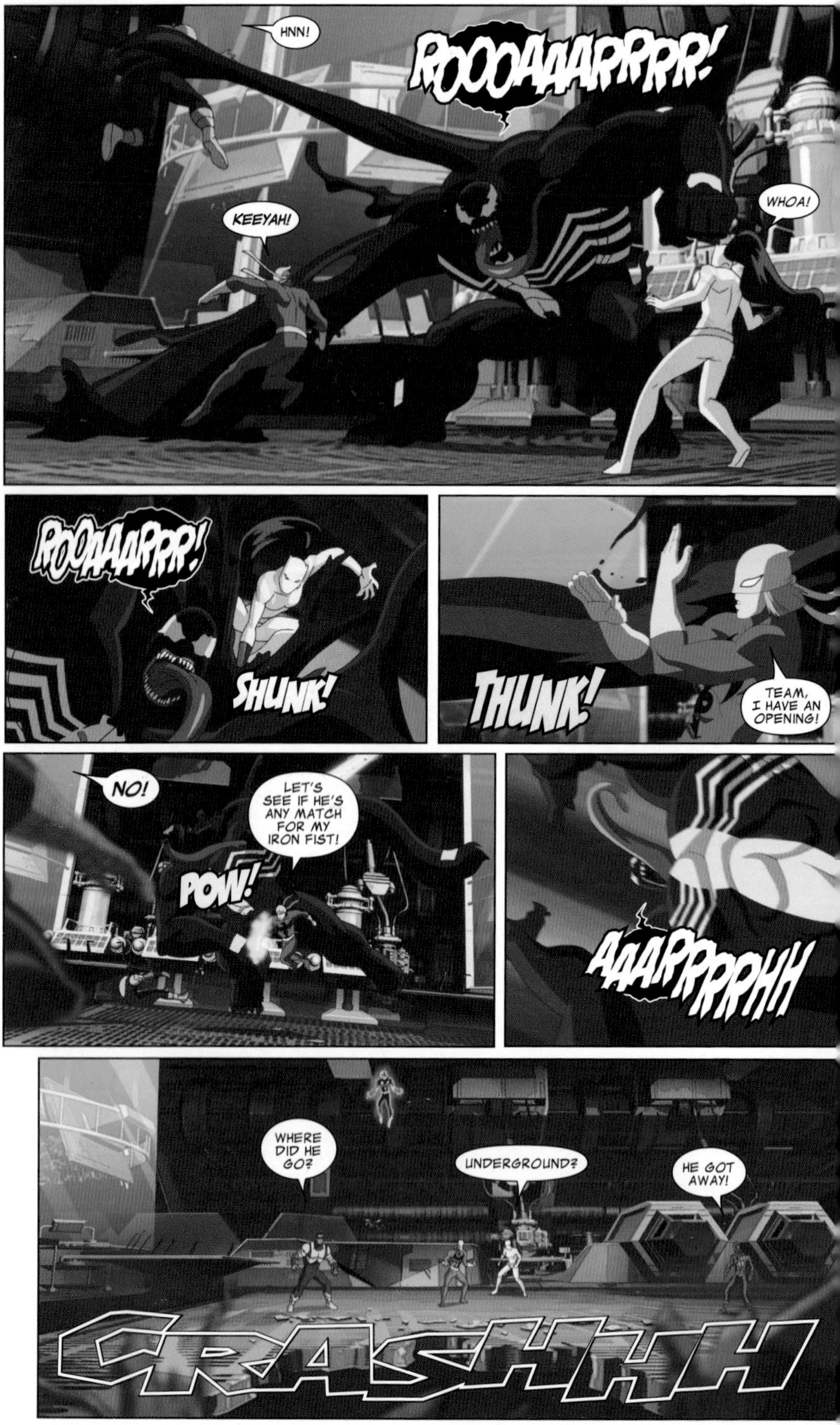

HNN!
ROOOAAARRRR!
KEEYAH!
WHOA!
ROOAAARRR!
SHUNK!
THUNK!
TEAM, I HAVE AN OPENING!
NO!
LET'S SEE IF HE'S ANY MATCH FOR MY IRON FIST!
POW!
AAARRRRHH
WHERE DID HE GO?
UNDERGROUND?
HE GOT AWAY!
CRASHHH

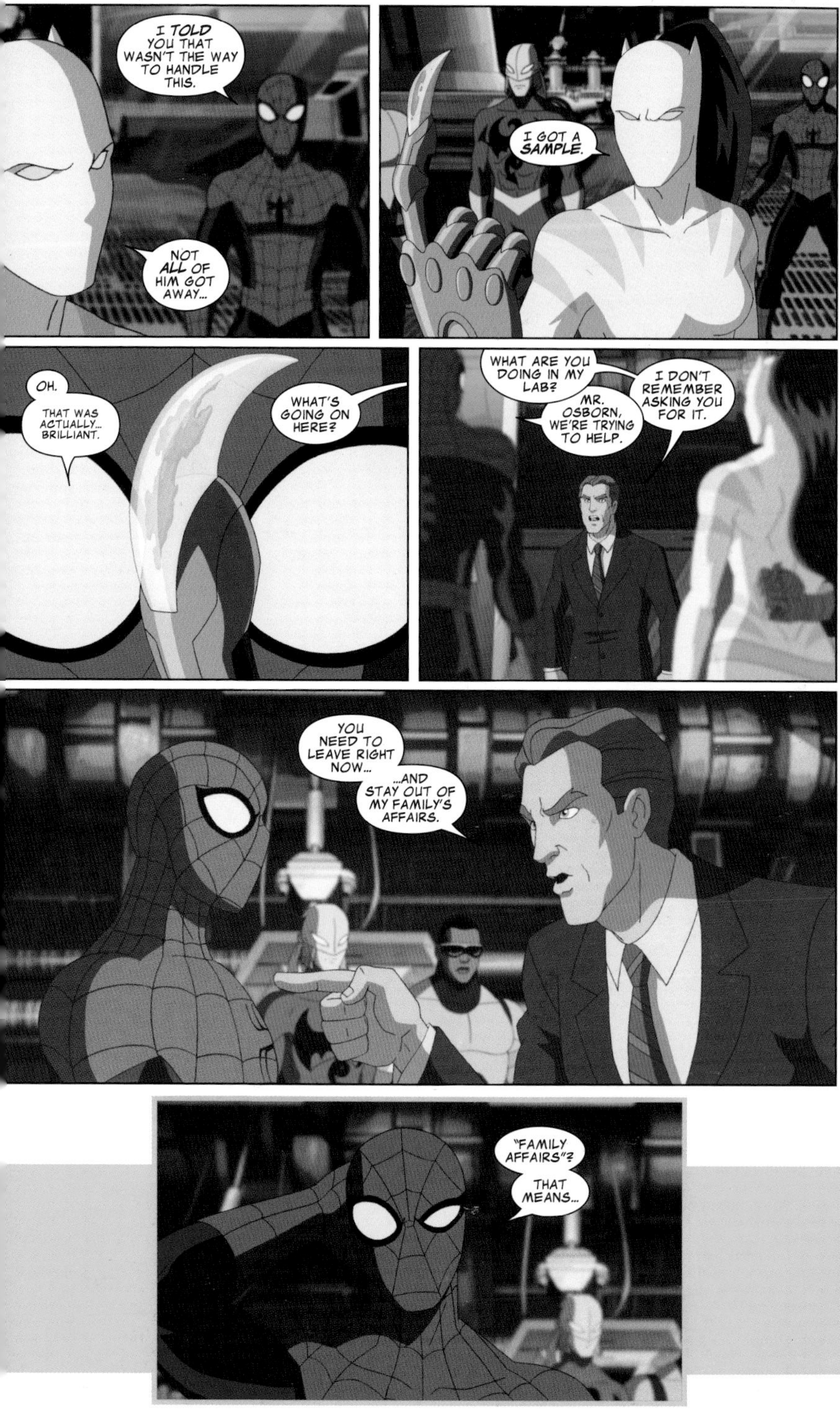
I TOLD YOU THAT WASN'T THE WAY TO HANDLE THIS.
NOT ALL OF HIM GOT AWAY...
I GOT A SAMPLE.
OH.
THAT WAS ACTUALLY... BRILLIANT.
WHAT'S GOING ON HERE?
WHAT ARE YOU DOING IN MY LAB?
MR. OSBORN, WE'RE TRYING TO HELP.
I DON'T REMEMBER ASKING YOU FOR IT.
YOU NEED TO LEAVE RIGHT NOW...
...AND STAY OUT OF MY FAMILY'S AFFAIRS.
"FAMILY AFFAIRS"?
THAT MEANS...

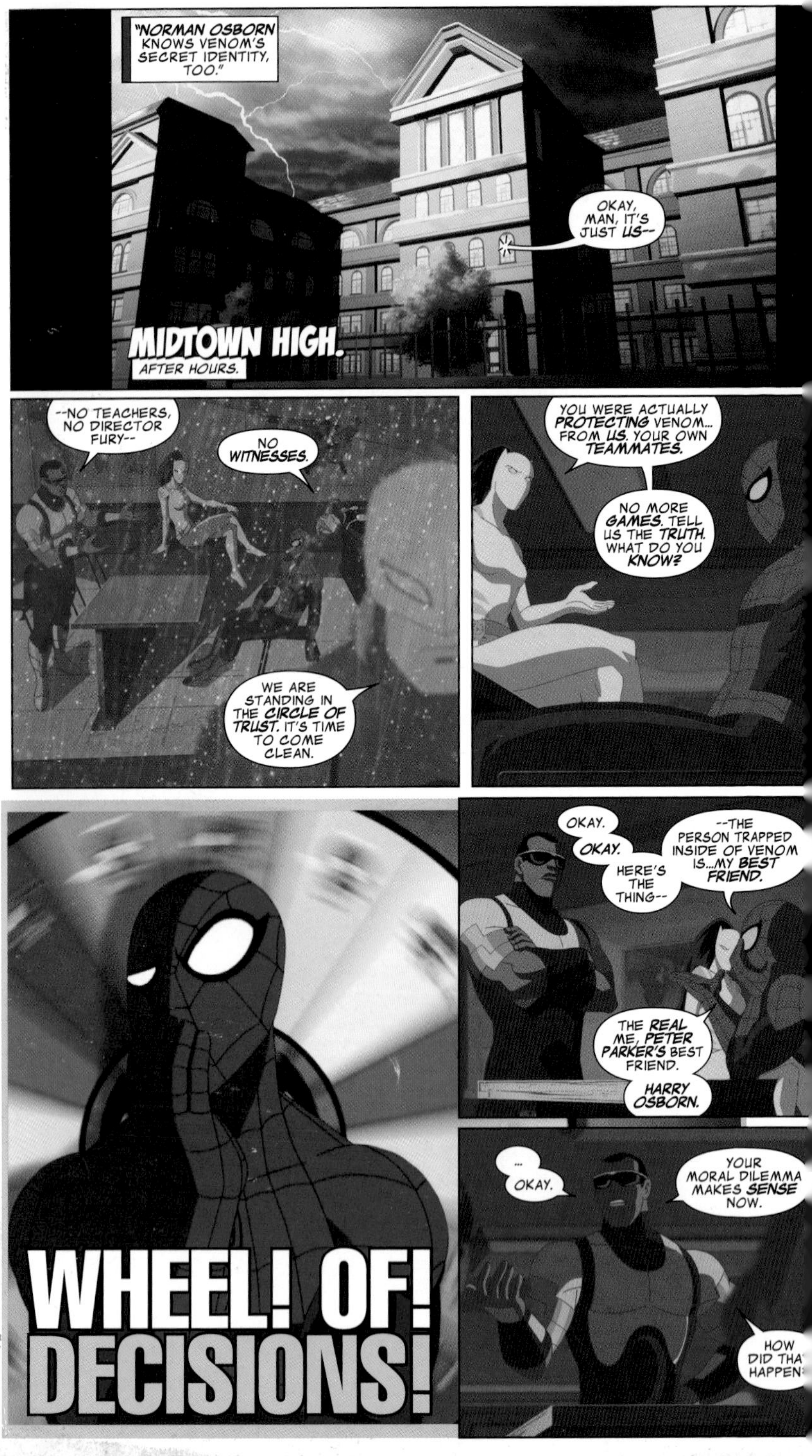
"NORMAN OSBORN KNOWS VENOM'S SECRET IDENTITY, TOO."
OKAY, MAN, IT'S JUST US--
MIDTOWN HIGH.
AFTER HOURS.
--NO TEACHERS, NO DIRECTOR FURY--
NO WITNESSES.
WE ARE STANDING IN THE CIRCLE OF TRUST. IT'S TIME TO COME CLEAN.
YOU WERE ACTUALLY PROTECTING VENOM... FROM US. YOUR OWN TEAMMATES.
NO MORE GAMES. TELL US THE TRUTH. WHAT DO YOU KNOW?
WHEEL! OF! DECISIONS!
OKAY.
OKAY.
HERE'S THE THING--
--THE PERSON TRAPPED INSIDE OF VENOM IS...MY BEST FRIEND.
THE REAL ME, PETER PARKER'S BEST FRIEND.
HARRY OSBORN.
... OKAY.
YOUR MORAL DILEMMA MAKES SENSE NOW.
HOW DID THAT HAPPEN?

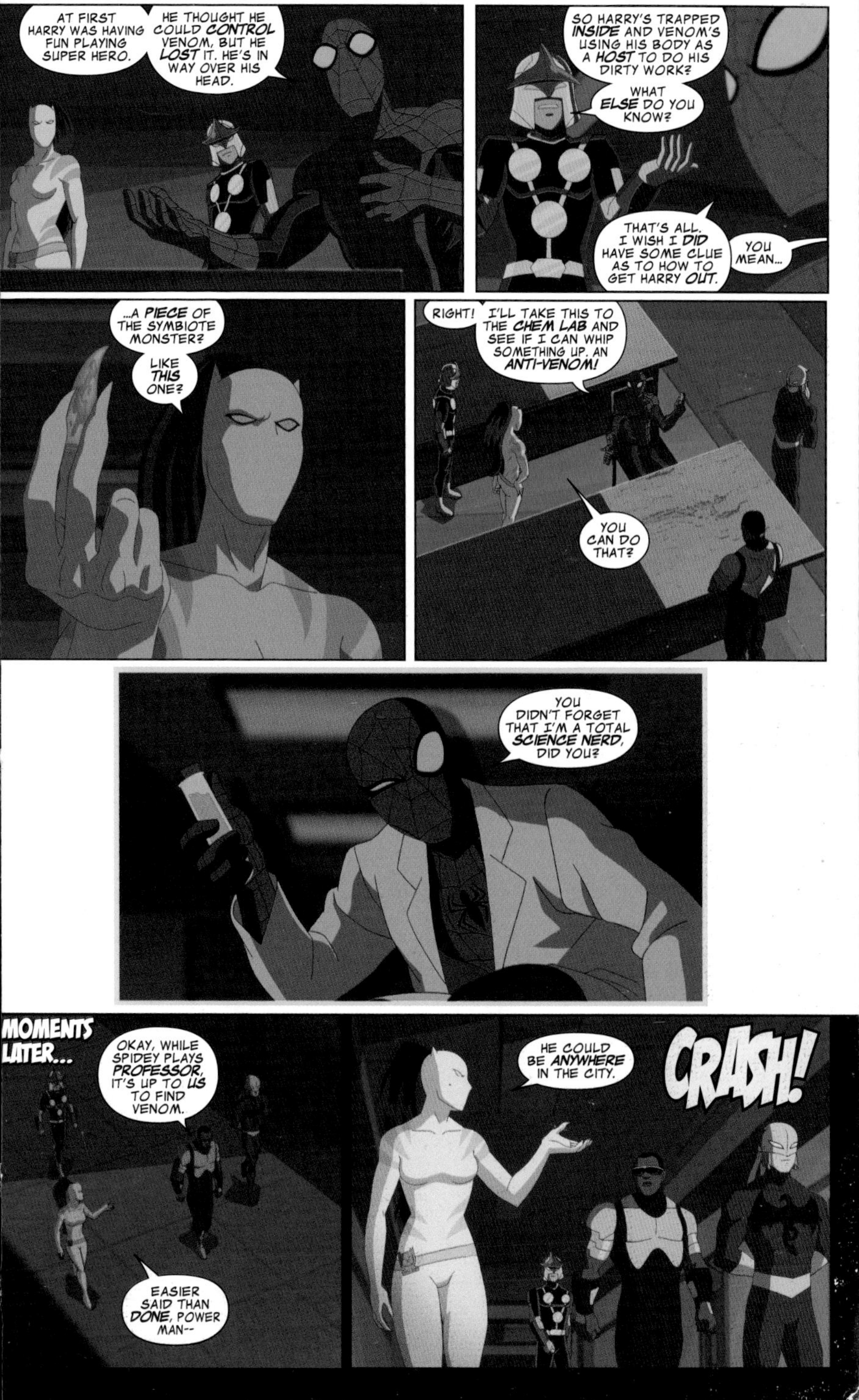

AT FIRST HARRY WAS HAVING FUN PLAYING SUPER HERO.
HE THOUGHT HE COULD CONTROL VENOM, BUT HE LOST IT. HE'S IN WAY OVER HIS HEAD.
SO HARRY'S TRAPPED INSIDE AND VENOM'S USING HIS BODY AS A HOST TO DO HIS DIRTY WORK?
WHAT ELSE DO YOU KNOW?
THAT'S ALL. I WISH I DID HAVE SOME CLUE AS TO HOW TO GET HARRY OUT.
YOU MEAN...
...A PIECE OF THE SYMBIOTE MONSTER?
LIKE THIS ONE?
RIGHT!
I'LL TAKE THIS TO THE CHEM LAB AND SEE IF I CAN WHIP SOMETHING UP. AN ANTI-VENOM!
YOU CAN DO THAT?
YOU DIDN'T FORGET THAT I'M A TOTAL SCIENCE NERD, DID YOU?
MOMENTS LATER...
OKAY, WHILE SPIDEY PLAYS PROFESSOR, IT'S UP TO US TO FIND VENOM.
EASIER SAID THAN DONE, POWER MAN--
HE COULD BE ANYWHERE IN THE CITY.
CRASH!

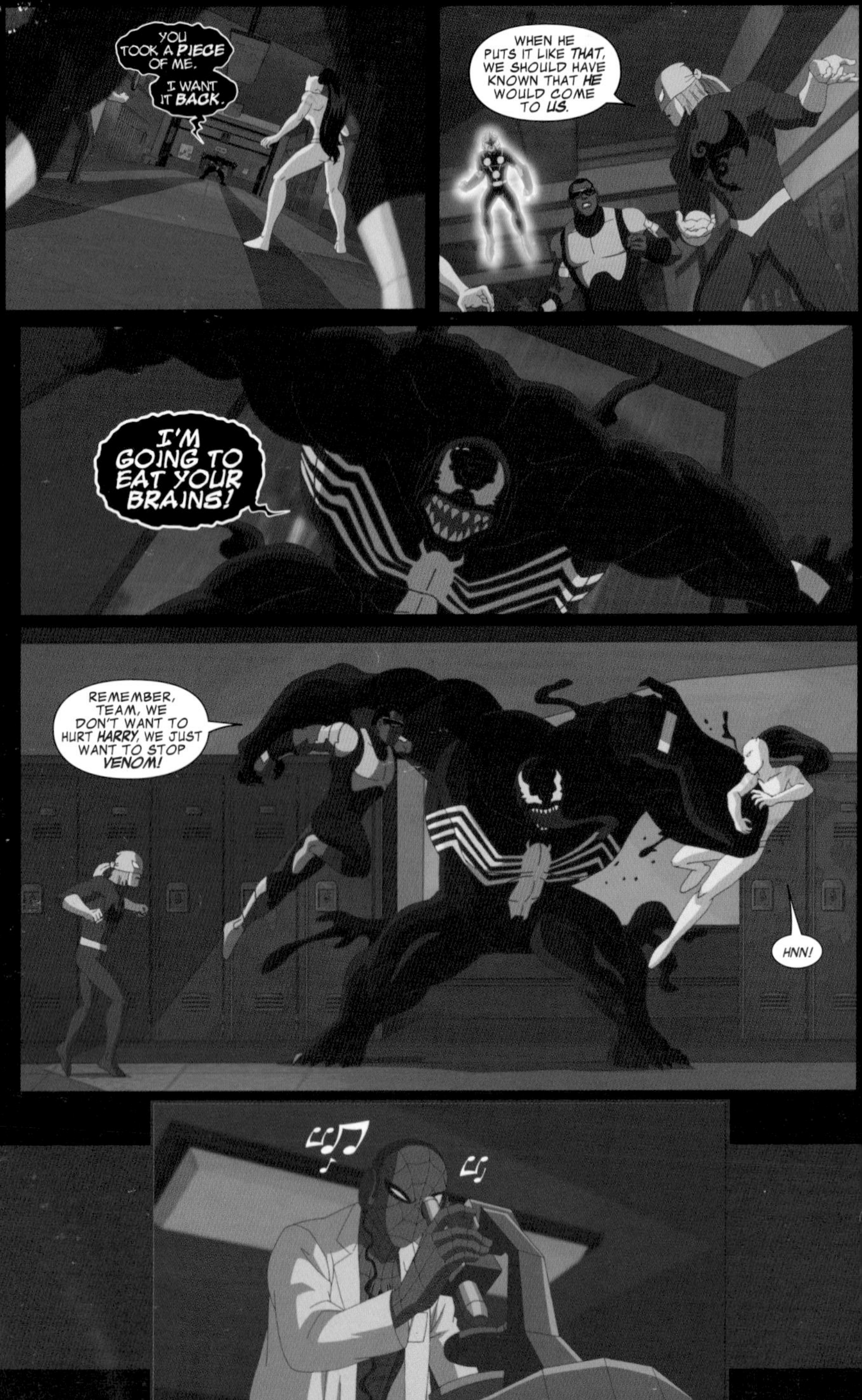
YOU TOOK A PIECE OF ME.
I WANT IT BACK.
WHEN HE PUTS IT LIKE THAT, WE SHOULD HAVE KNOWN THAT HE WOULD COME TO US.
I'M GOING TO EAT YOUR BRAINS!
REMEMBER, TEAM, WE DON'T WANT TO HURT HARRY, WE JUST WANT TO STOP VENOM!
HNN!

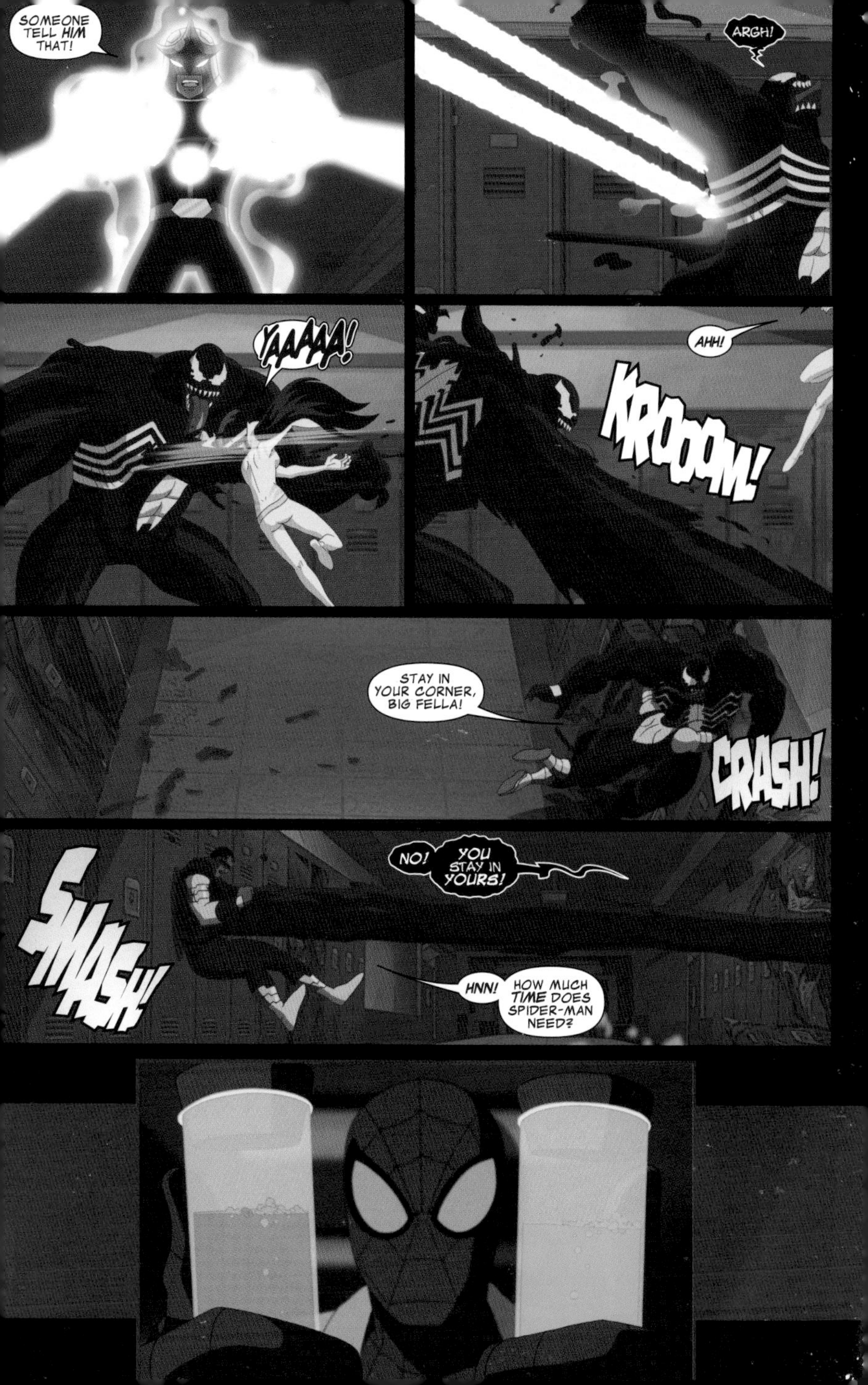
SOMEONE TELL HIM THAT!
ARGH!
YAAAAA!
AHH!
KROOOM!
STAY IN YOUR CORNER, BIG FELLA!
CRASH!
SMASH!
NO!
YOU STAY IN YOURS!
HNN!
HOW MUCH TIME DOES SPIDER-MAN NEED?

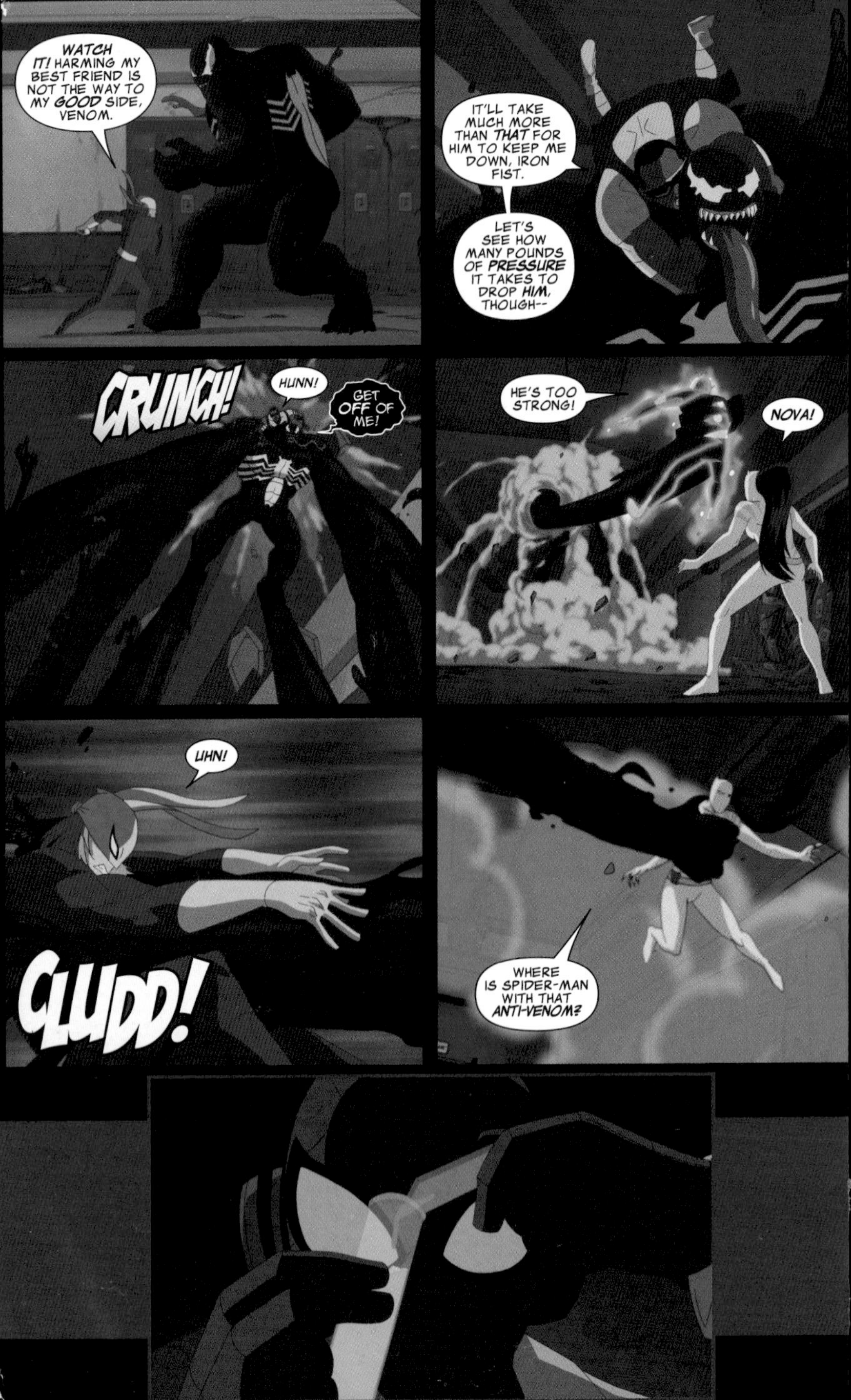
WATCH IT! HARMING MY BEST FRIEND IS NOT THE WAY TO MY GOOD SIDE, VENOM.
IT'LL TAKE MUCH MORE THAN THAT FOR HIM TO KEEP ME DOWN, IRON FIST.
LET'S SEE HOW MANY POUNDS OF PRESSURE IT TAKES TO DROP HIM, THOUGH--
CRUNCH!
HUNN!
GET OFF OF ME!
HE'S TOO STRONG!
NOVA!
UHN!
CLUDD!
WHERE IS SPIDER-MAN WITH THAT ANTI-VENOM?

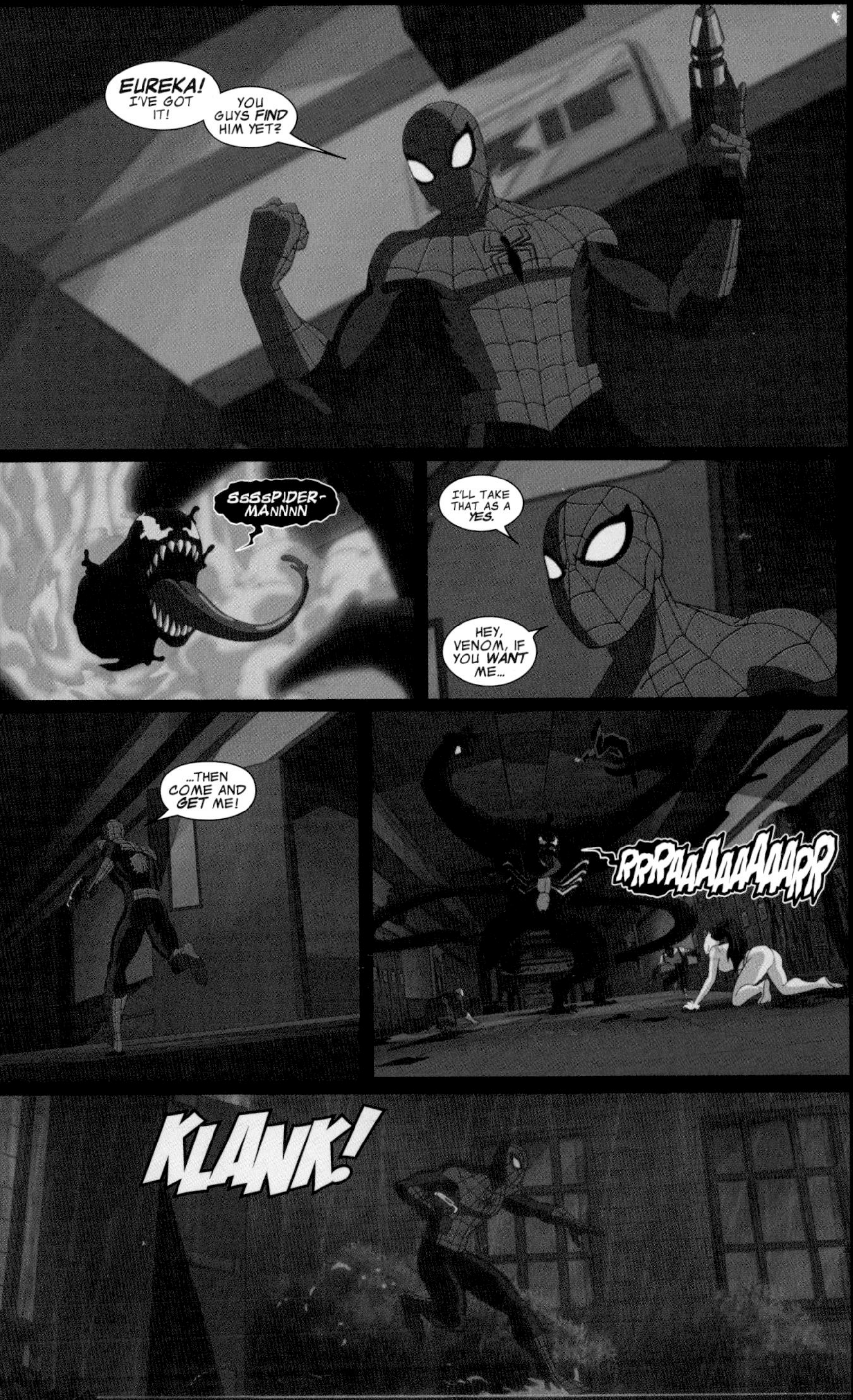
EUREKA! I'VE GOT IT!
YOU GUYS FIND HIM YET?
SsSsSPIDER-MANNNN
I'LL TAKE THAT AS A YES.
HEY, VENOM, IF YOU WANT ME...
...THEN COME AND GET ME!
RRRAAAAAAAARR
KLANK!

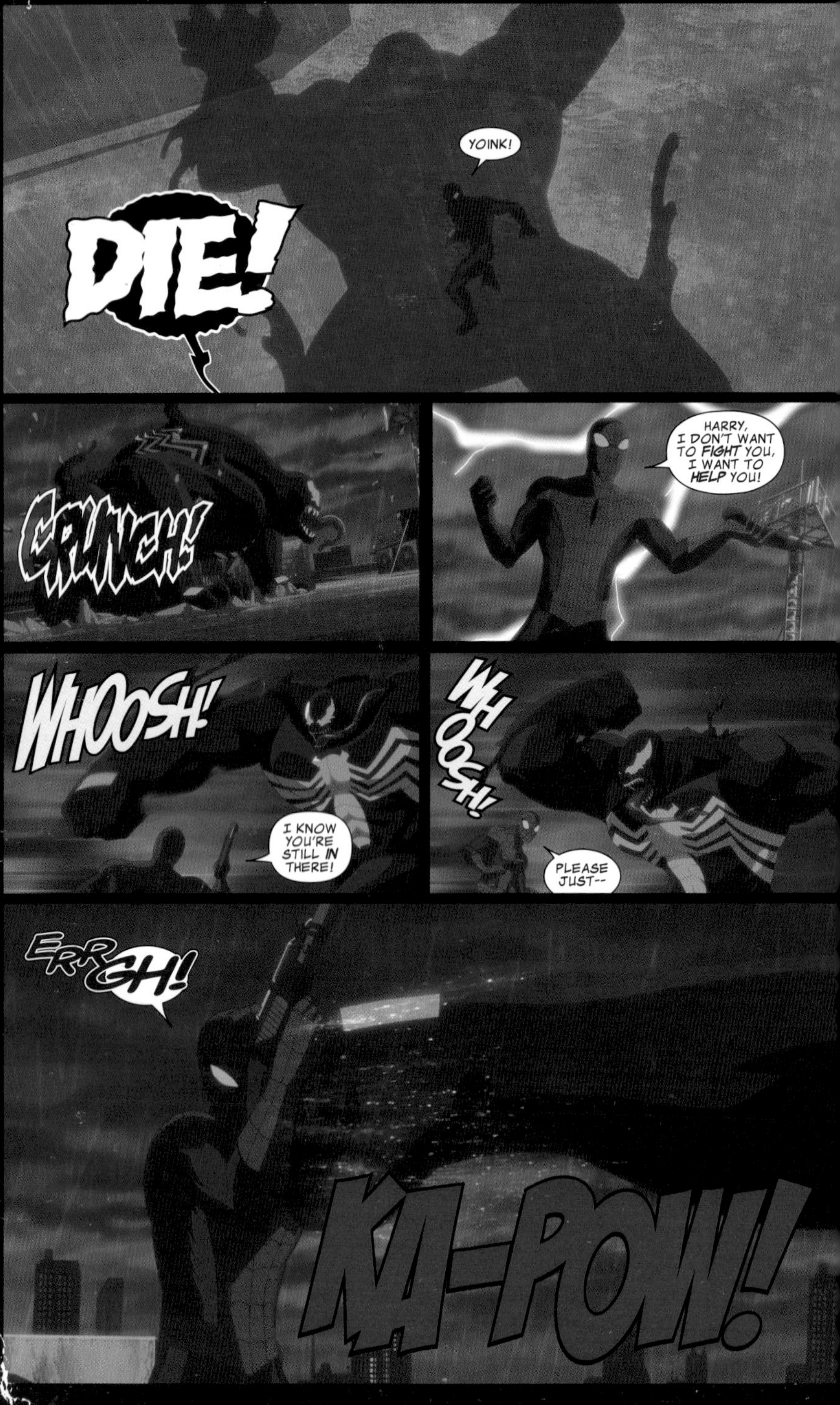
YOINK!
DIE!
CRUNCH!
HARRY, I DON'T WANT TO FIGHT YOU, I WANT TO HELP YOU!
WHOOSH!
I KNOW YOU'RE STILL IN THERE!
WHOOSH!
PLEASE JUST--
ERRGH!
KA-POW!

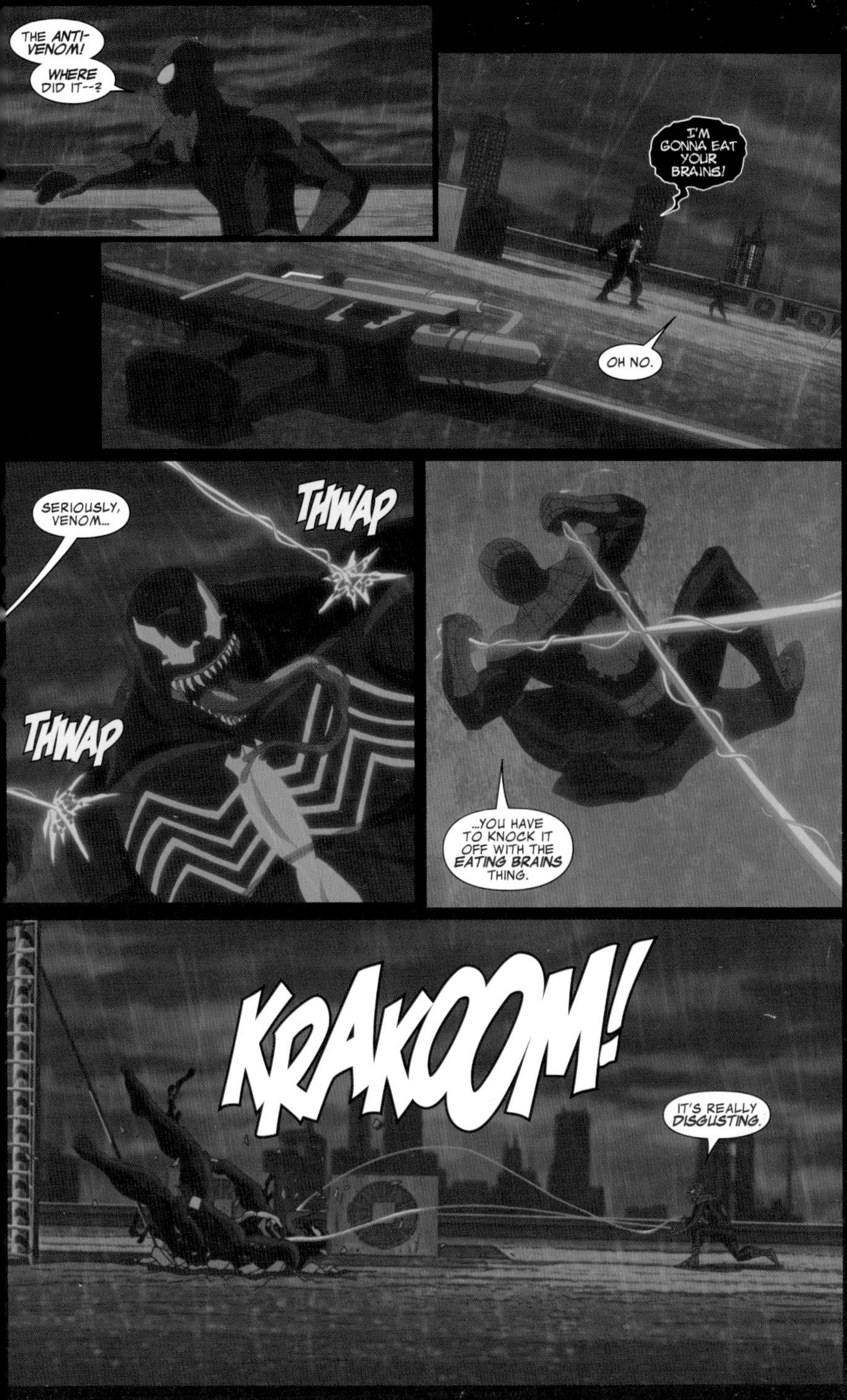
THE ANTI-VENOM!
WHERE DID IT--?
I'M GONNA EAT YOUR BRAINS!
OH NO.
SERIOUSLY, VENOM...
THWAP
THWAP
...YOU HAVE TO KNOCK IT OFF WITH THE EATING BRAINS THING.
KRAKOOM!
IT'S REALLY DISGUSTING.

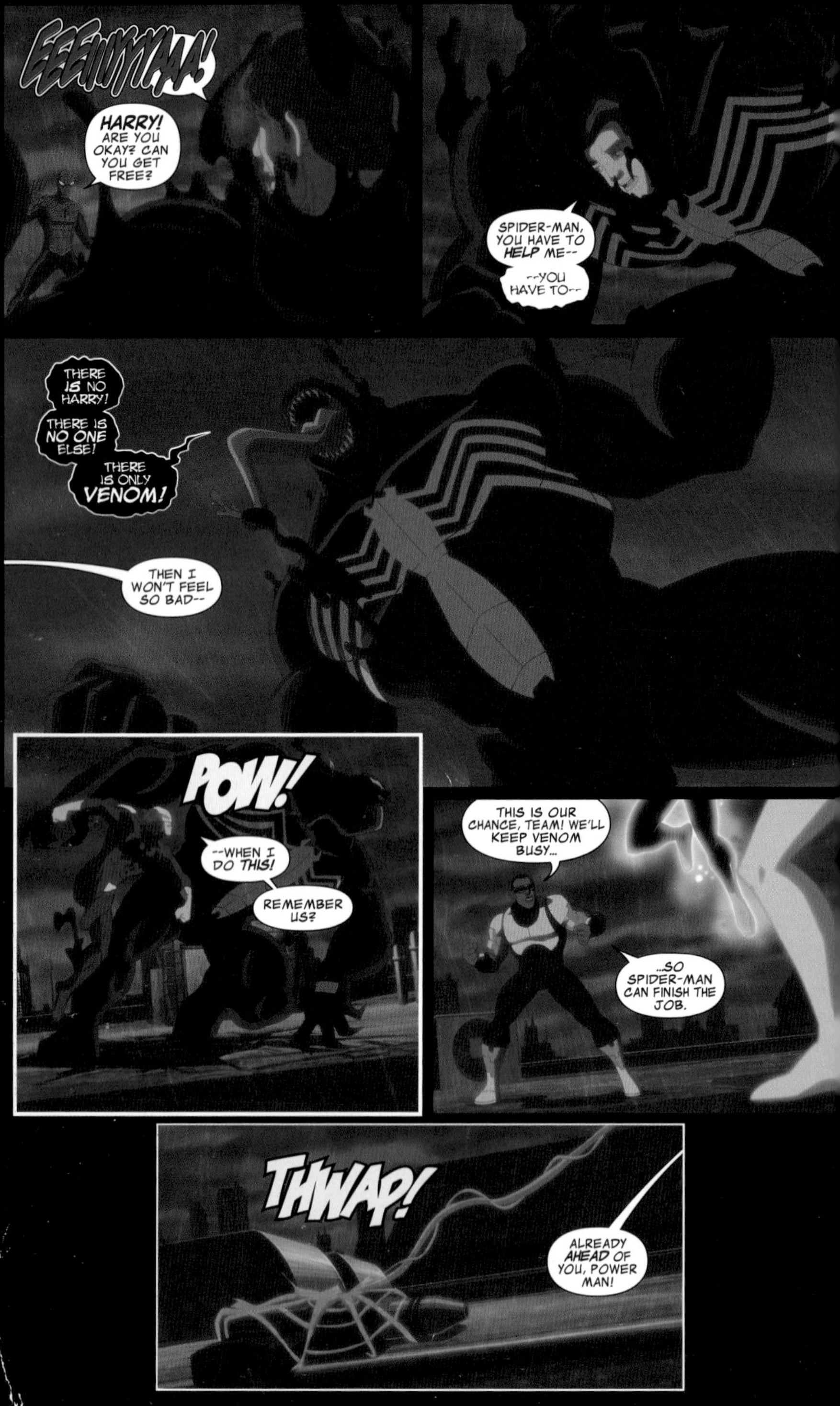
EEEIIIYYYAAA!
HARRY! ARE YOU OKAY? CAN YOU GET FREE?
SPIDER-MAN, YOU HAVE TO HELP ME--
--YOU HAVE TO--
THERE IS NO HARRY!
THERE IS NO ONE ELSE!
THERE IS ONLY VENOM!
THEN I WON'T FEEL SO BAD--
POW!
--WHEN I DO THIS!
REMEMBER US?
THIS IS OUR CHANCE, TEAM! WE'LL KEEP VENOM BUSY...
...SO SPIDER-MAN CAN FINISH THE JOB.
THWAP!
ALREADY AHEAD OF YOU, POWER MAN!

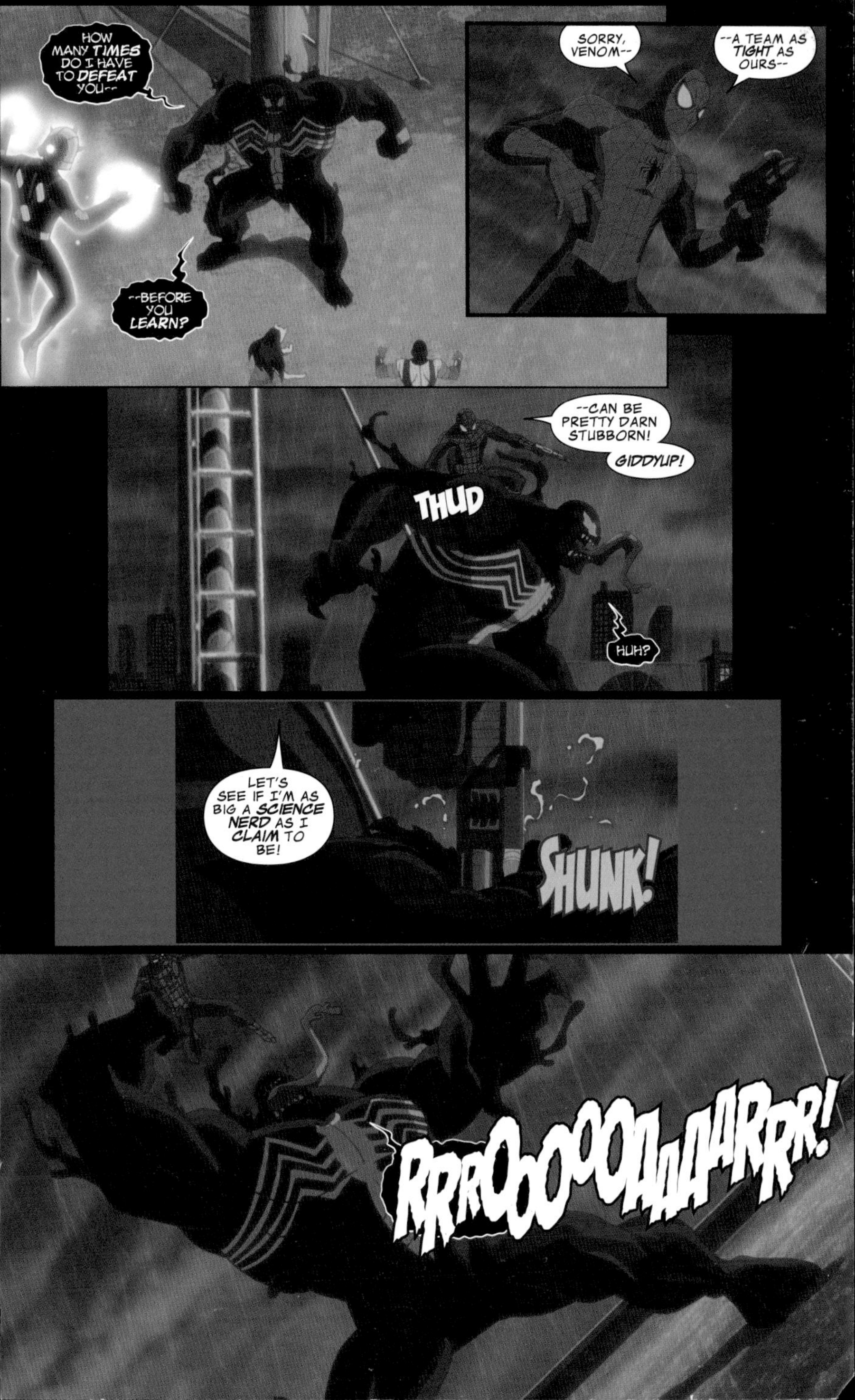
HOW MANY TIMES DO I HAVE TO DEFEAT YOU--
--BEFORE YOU LEARN?
SORRY, VENOM--
--A TEAM AS TIGHT AS OURS--
--CAN BE PRETTY DARN STUBBORN!
GIDDYUP!
THUD
HUH?
LET'S SEE IF I'M AS BIG A SCIENCE NERD AS I CLAIM TO BE!
SHUNK!
RRROOOOAAARRR!

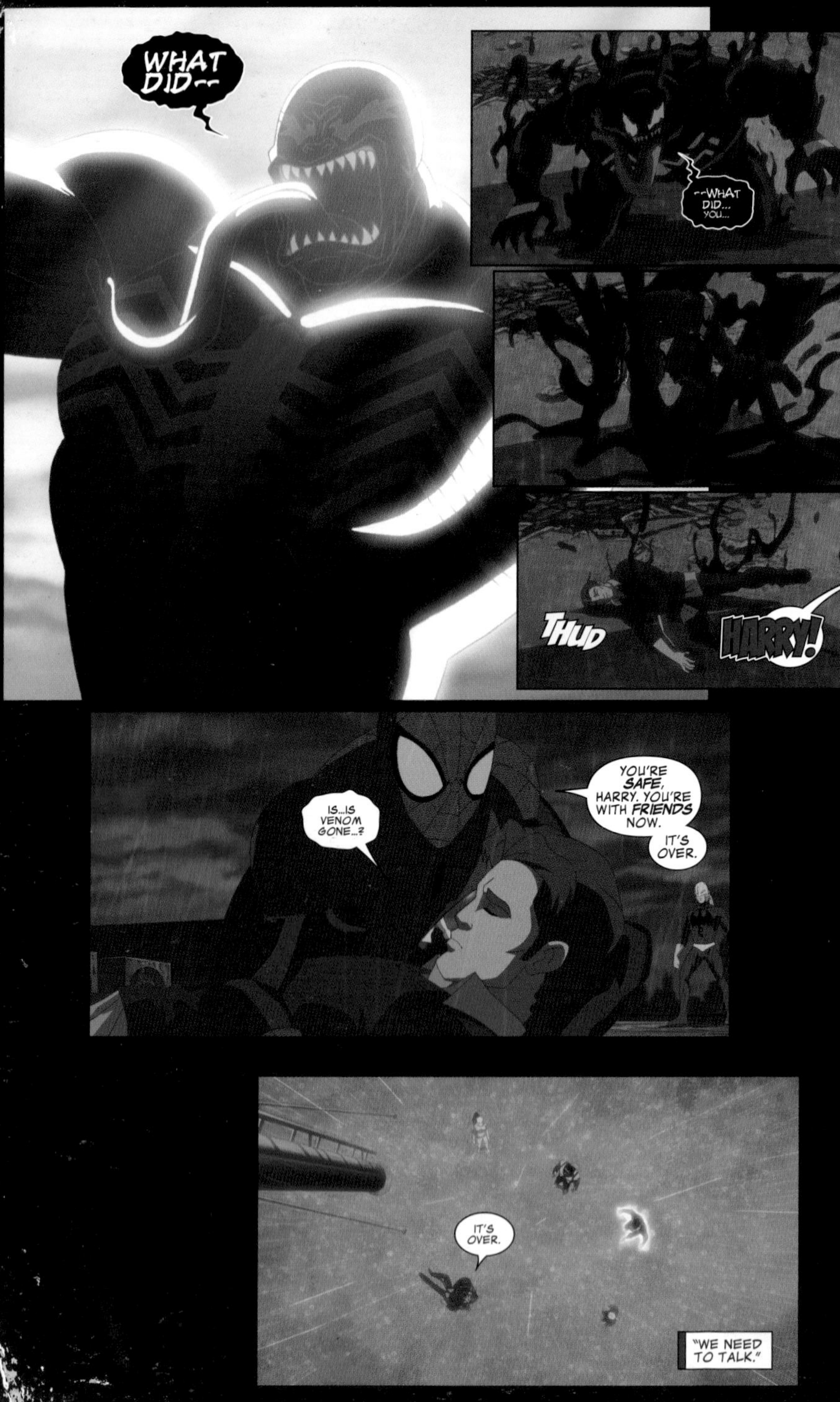
WHAT DID--
--WHAT DID... YOU...
THUD
HARRY!
IS...IS VENOM GONE...?
YOU'RE SAFE, HARRY. YOU'RE WITH FRIENDS NOW.
IT'S OVER.
IT'S OVER.
"WE NEED TO TALK."

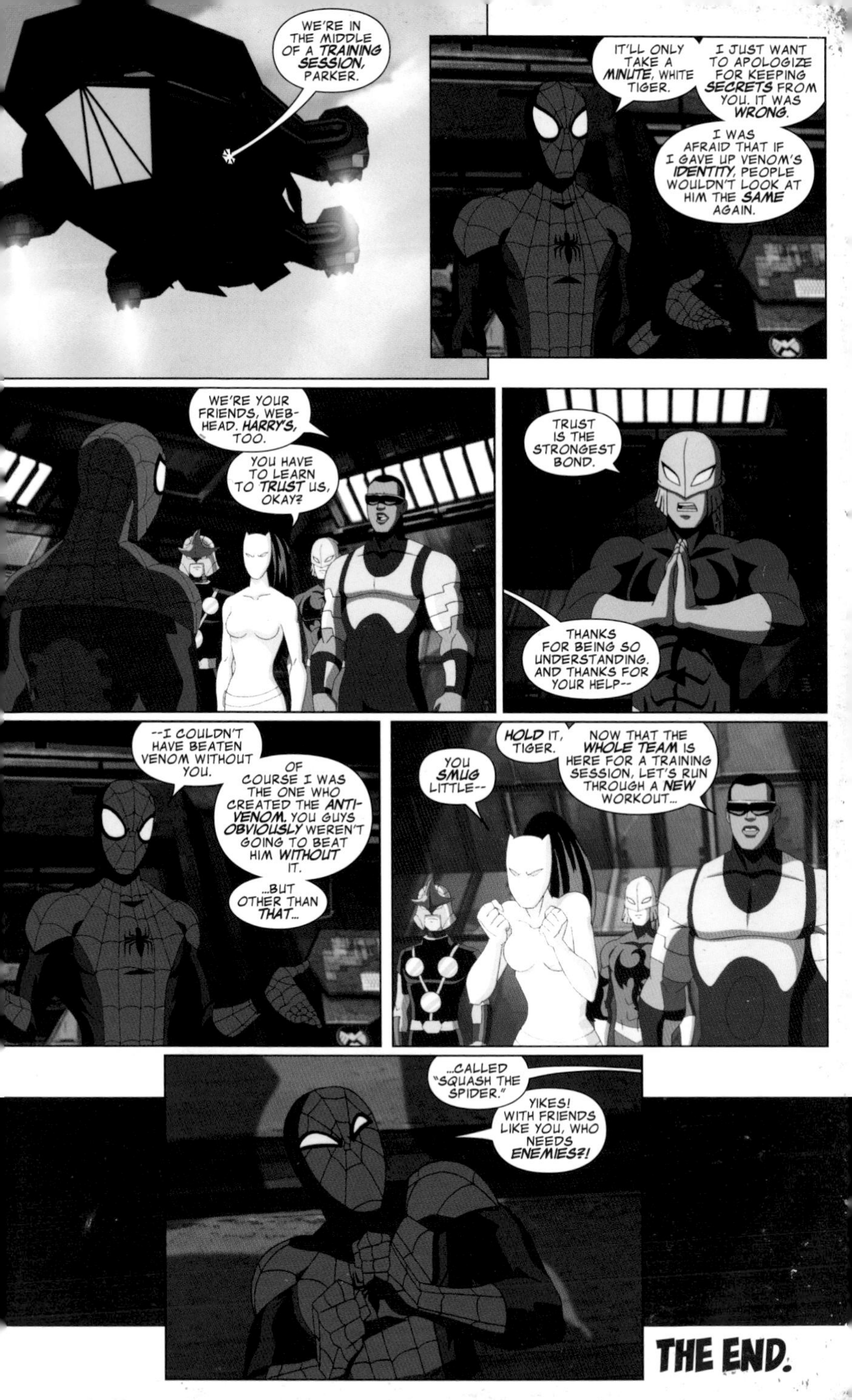
WE'RE IN THE MIDDLE OF A TRAINING SESSION, PARKER.
IT'LL ONLY TAKE A MINUTE, WHITE TIGER.
I JUST WANT TO APOLOGIZE FOR KEEPING SECRETS FROM YOU. IT WAS WRONG.
I WAS AFRAID THAT IF I GAVE UP VENOM'S IDENTITY, PEOPLE WOULDN'T LOOK AT HIM THE SAME AGAIN.
WE'RE YOUR FRIENDS, WEB-HEAD. HARRY'S, TOO.
YOU HAVE TO LEARN TO TRUST US, OKAY?
TRUST IS THE STRONGEST BOND.
THANKS FOR BEING SO UNDERSTANDING. AND THANKS FOR YOUR HELP--
--I COULDN'T HAVE BEATEN VENOM WITHOUT YOU.
OF COURSE I WAS THE ONE WHO CREATED THE ANTI-VENOM. YOU GUYS OBVIOUSLY WEREN'T GOING TO BEAT HIM WITHOUT IT.
...BUT OTHER THAN THAT...
YOU SMUG LITTLE--
HOLD IT, TIGER.
NOW THAT THE WHOLE TEAM IS HERE FOR A TRAINING SESSION, LET'S RUN THROUGH A NEW WORKOUT...
...CALLED "SQUASH THE SPIDER."
YIKES! WITH FRIENDS LIKE YOU, WHO NEEDS ENEMIES?!
THE END.

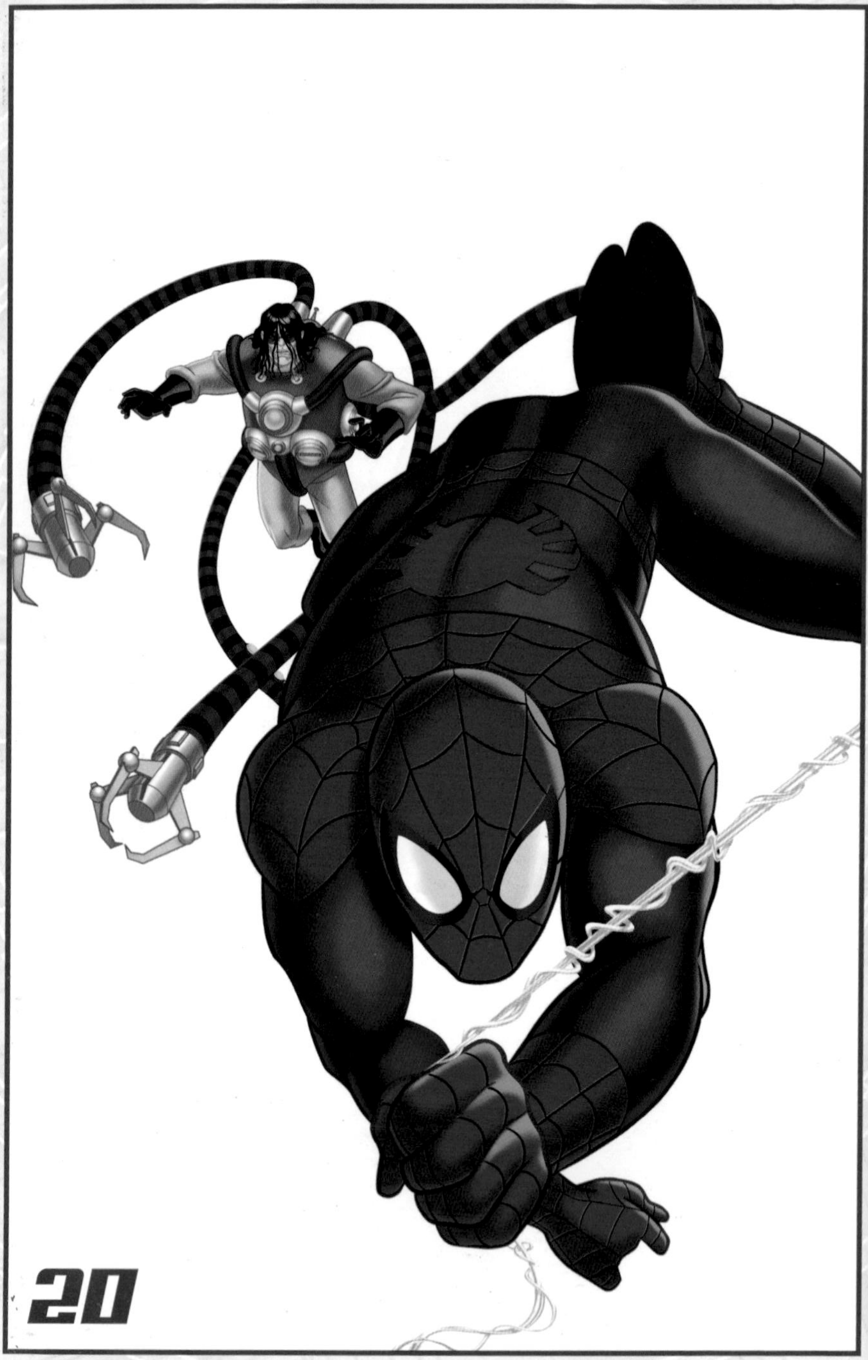
20

Based on **"Me Time"**

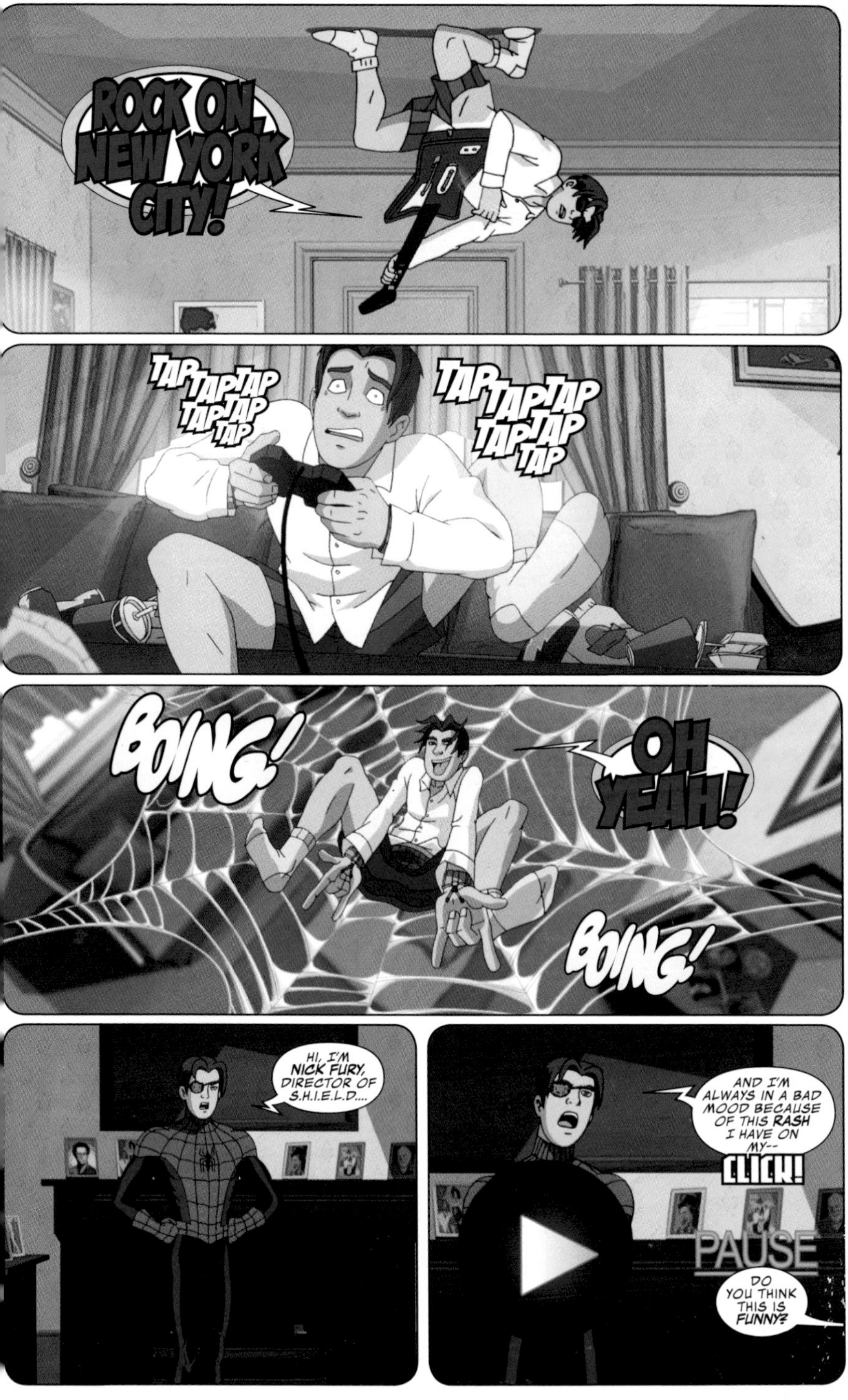
ROCK ON, NEW YORK CITY!
TAP TAP TAP TAP TAP TAP
TAP TAP TAP TAP TAP TAP
BOING!
OH YEAH!
BOING!
HI, I'M NICK FURY, DIRECTOR OF S.H.I.E.L.D....
AND I'M ALWAYS IN A BAD MOOD BECAUSE OF THIS RASH I HAVE ON MY--
CLICK!
PAUSE
DO YOU THINK THIS IS FUNNY?

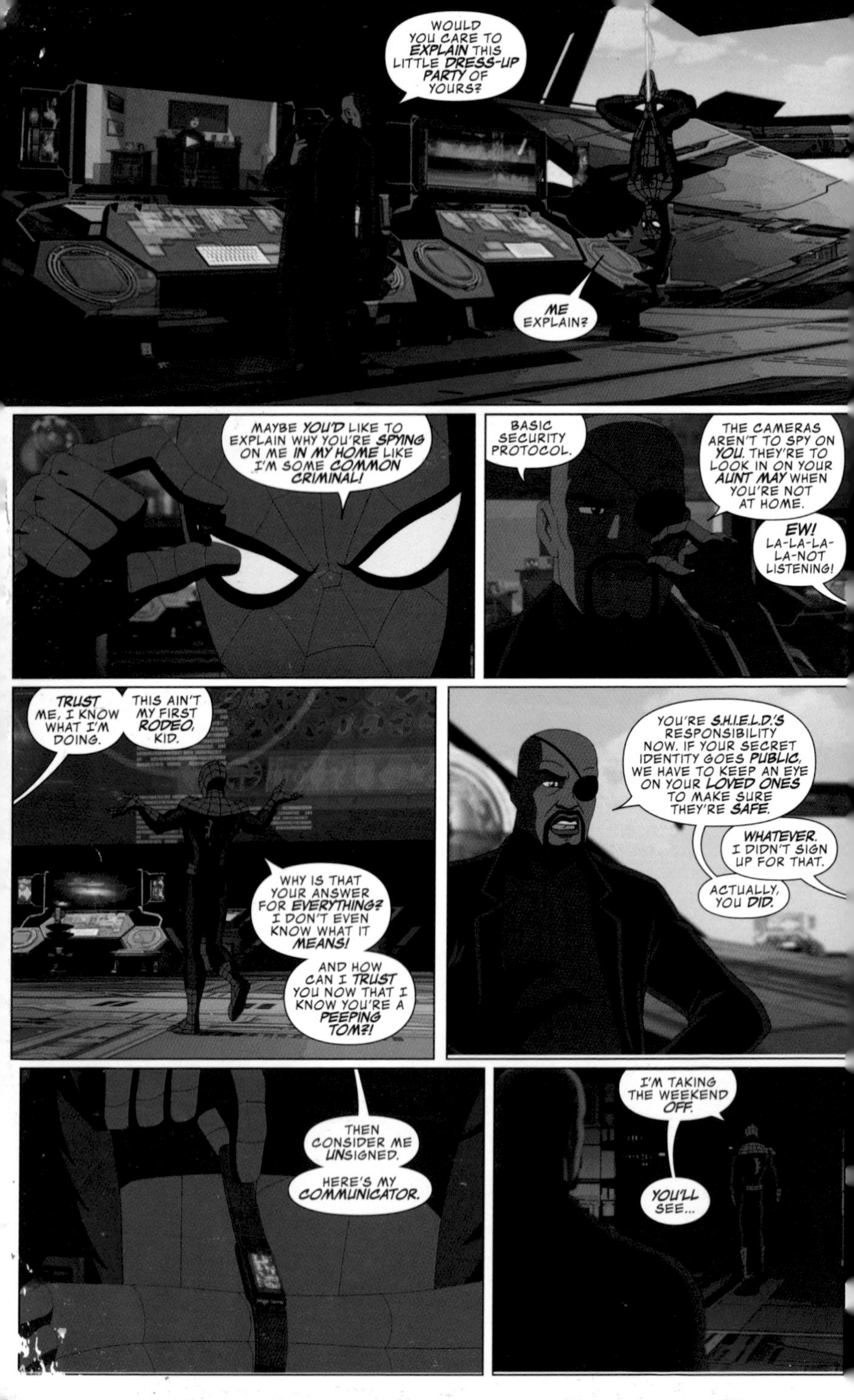
WOULD YOU CARE TO EXPLAIN THIS LITTLE DRESS-UP PARTY OF YOURS?
ME EXPLAIN?
MAYBE YOU'D LIKE TO EXPLAIN WHY YOU'RE SPYING ON ME IN MY HOME LIKE I'M SOME COMMON CRIMINAL!
BASIC SECURITY PROTOCOL.
THE CAMERAS AREN'T TO SPY ON YOU. THEY'RE TO LOOK IN ON YOUR AUNT MAY WHEN YOU'RE NOT AT HOME.
EW! LA-LA-LA-LA-NOT LISTENING!
TRUST ME, I KNOW WHAT I'M DOING.
THIS AIN'T MY FIRST RODEO, KID.
WHY IS THAT YOUR ANSWER FOR EVERYTHING? I DON'T EVEN KNOW WHAT IT MEANS!
AND HOW CAN I TRUST YOU NOW THAT I KNOW YOU'RE A PEEPING TOM?!
YOU'RE S.H.I.E.L.D.'S RESPONSIBILITY NOW. IF YOUR SECRET IDENTITY GOES PUBLIC, WE HAVE TO KEEP AN EYE ON YOUR LOVED ONES TO MAKE SURE THEY'RE SAFE.
WHATEVER. I DIDN'T SIGN UP FOR THAT.
ACTUALLY, YOU DID.
THEN CONSIDER ME UNSIGNED.
HERE'S MY COMMUNICATOR.
I'M TAKING THE WEEKEND OFF.
YOU'LL SEE...

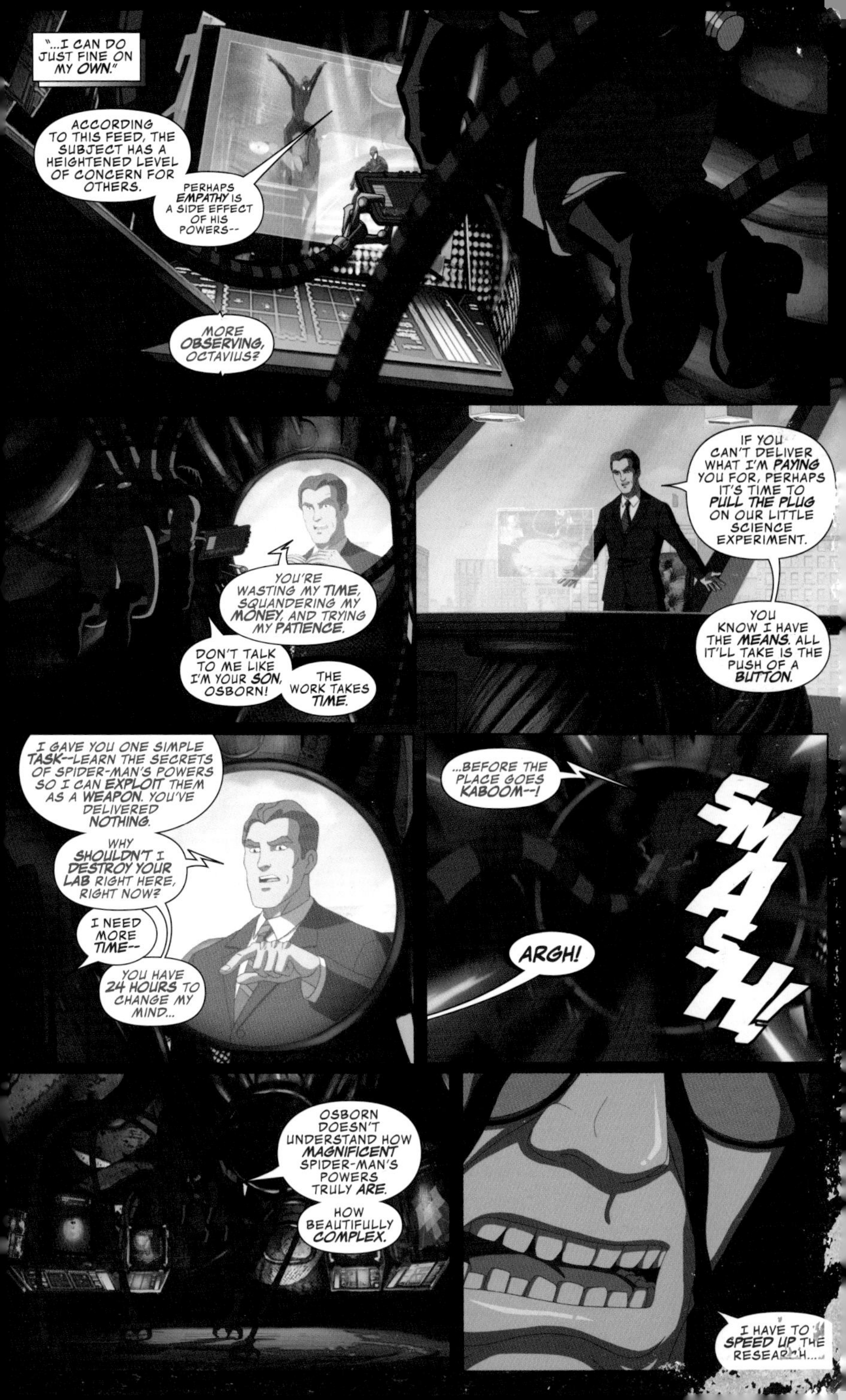
"...I CAN DO JUST FINE ON MY OWN."
ACCORDING TO THIS FEED, THE SUBJECT HAS A HEIGHTENED LEVEL OF CONCERN FOR OTHERS.
PERHAPS EMPATHY IS A SIDE EFFECT OF HIS POWERS--
MORE OBSERVING, OCTAVIUS?
YOU'RE WASTING MY TIME, SQUANDERING MY MONEY, AND TRYING MY PATIENCE.
DON'T TALK TO ME LIKE I'M YOUR SON, OSBORN!
THE WORK TAKES TIME.
IF YOU CAN'T DELIVER WHAT I'M PAYING YOU FOR, PERHAPS IT'S TIME TO PULL THE PLUG ON OUR LITTLE SCIENCE EXPERIMENT.
YOU KNOW I HAVE THE MEANS. ALL IT'LL TAKE IS THE PUSH OF A BUTTON.
I GAVE YOU ONE SIMPLE TASK--LEARN THE SECRETS OF SPIDER-MAN'S POWERS SO I CAN EXPLOIT THEM AS A WEAPON. YOU'VE DELIVERED NOTHING.
WHY SHOULDN'T I DESTROY YOUR LAB RIGHT HERE, RIGHT NOW?
I NEED MORE TIME--
YOU HAVE 24 HOURS TO CHANGE MY MIND...
...BEFORE THE PLACE GOES KABOOM--!
SMASH!
ARGH!
OSBORN DOESN'T UNDERSTAND HOW MAGNIFICENT SPIDER-MAN'S POWERS TRULY ARE.
HOW BEAUTIFULLY COMPLEX.
I HAVE TO SPEED UP THE RESEARCH....

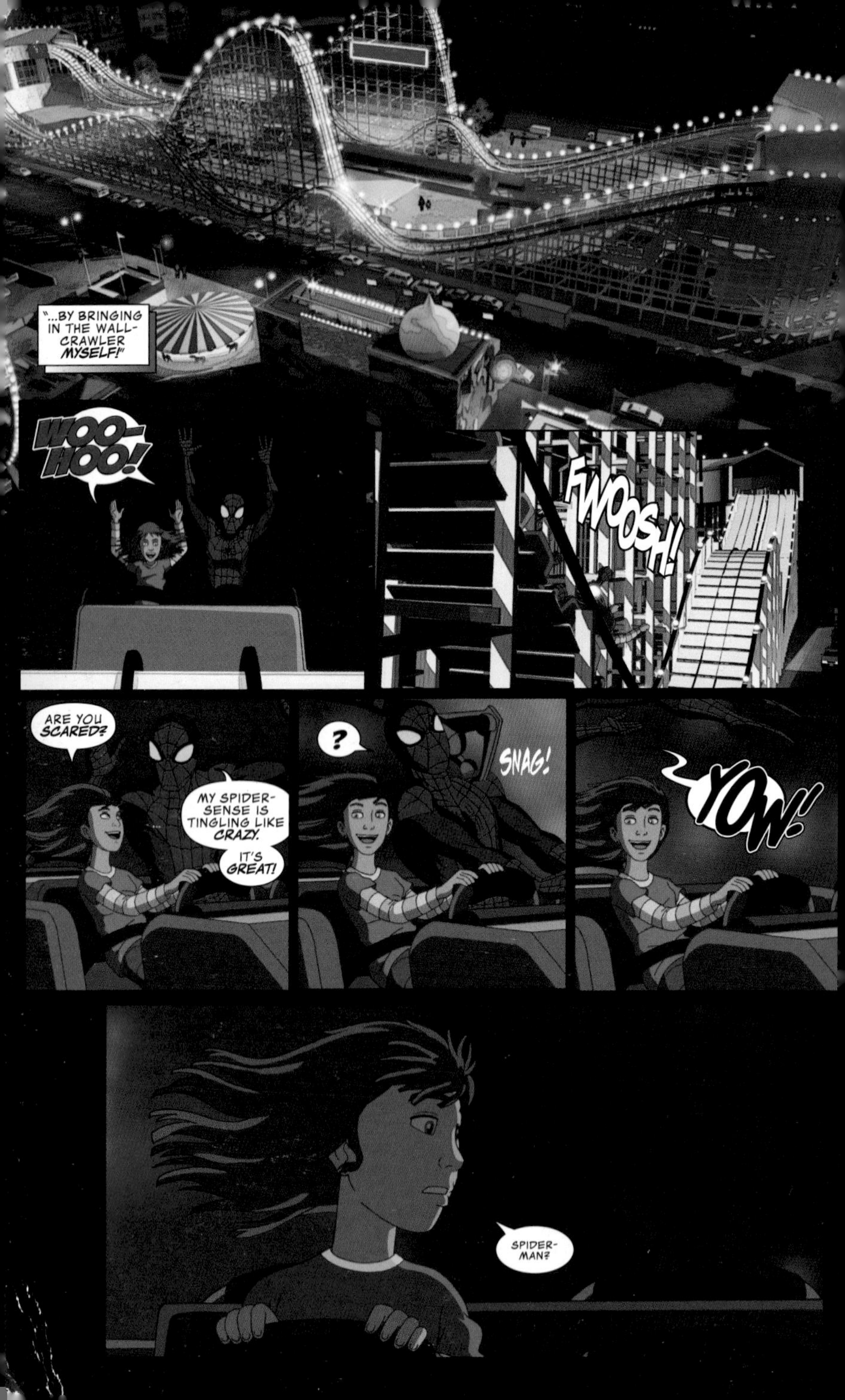
"...BY BRINGING IN THE WALL-CRAWLER *MYSELF!*"
WOO-HOO!
FWOOSH!
ARE YOU *SCARED?*
MY SPIDER-SENSE IS TINGLING LIKE *CRAZY.*
IT'S *GREAT!*
?
SNAG!
YOW!
SPIDER-MAN?

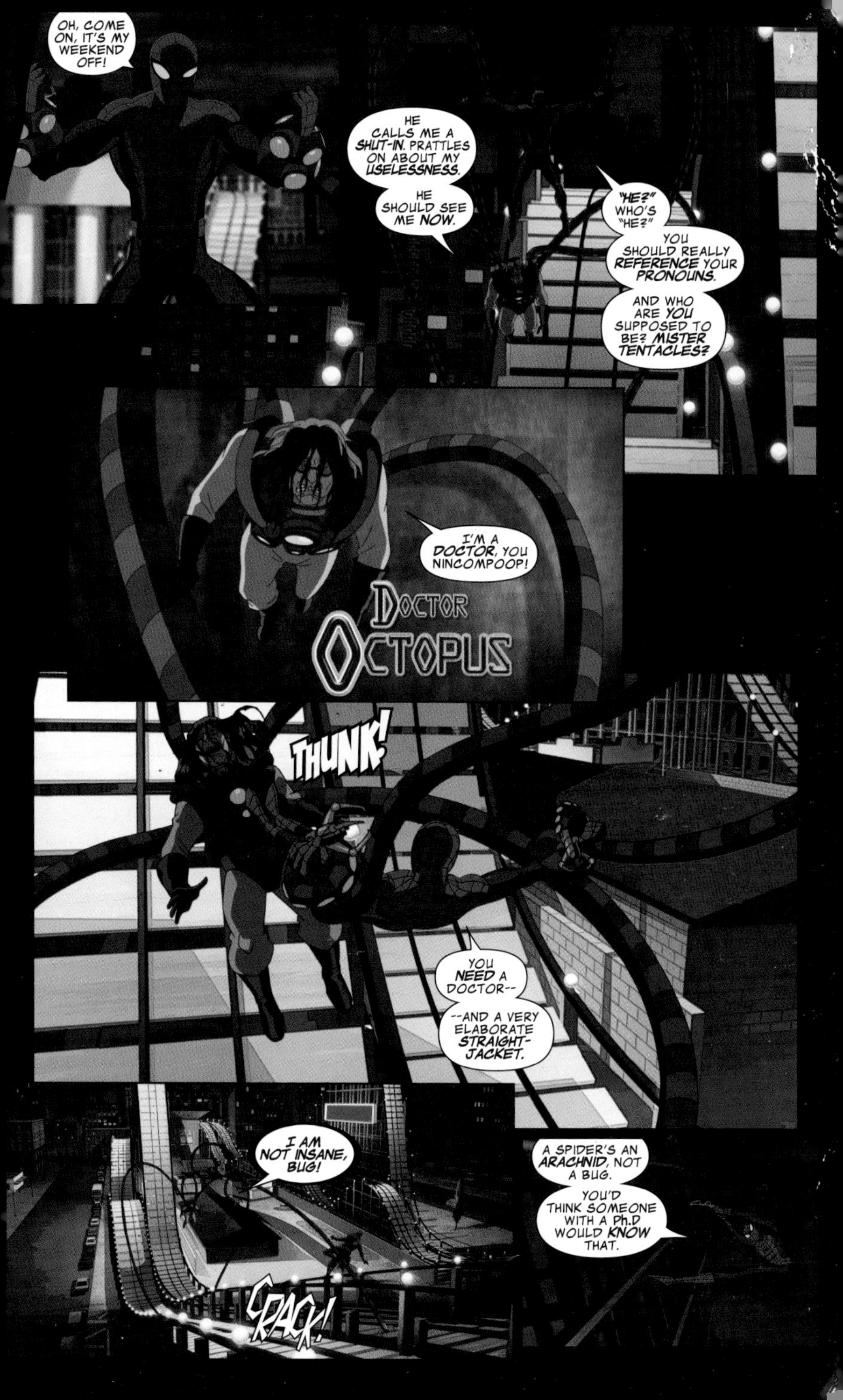
OH, COME ON, IT'S MY WEEKEND OFF!
HE CALLS ME A SHUT-IN. PRATTLES ON ABOUT MY USELESSNESS.
HE SHOULD SEE ME NOW.
"HE?" WHO'S "HE?"
YOU SHOULD REALLY REFERENCE YOUR PRONOUNS.
AND WHO ARE YOU SUPPOSED TO BE? MISTER TENTACLES?
I'M A DOCTOR, YOU NINCOMPOOP!
DOCTOR OCTOPUS
THUNK!
YOU NEED A DOCTOR--
--AND A VERY ELABORATE STRAIGHT-JACKET.
I AM NOT INSANE, BUG!
A SPIDER'S AN ARACHNID, NOT A BUG.
YOU'D THINK SOMEONE WITH A Ph.D WOULD KNOW THAT.
CRACK!

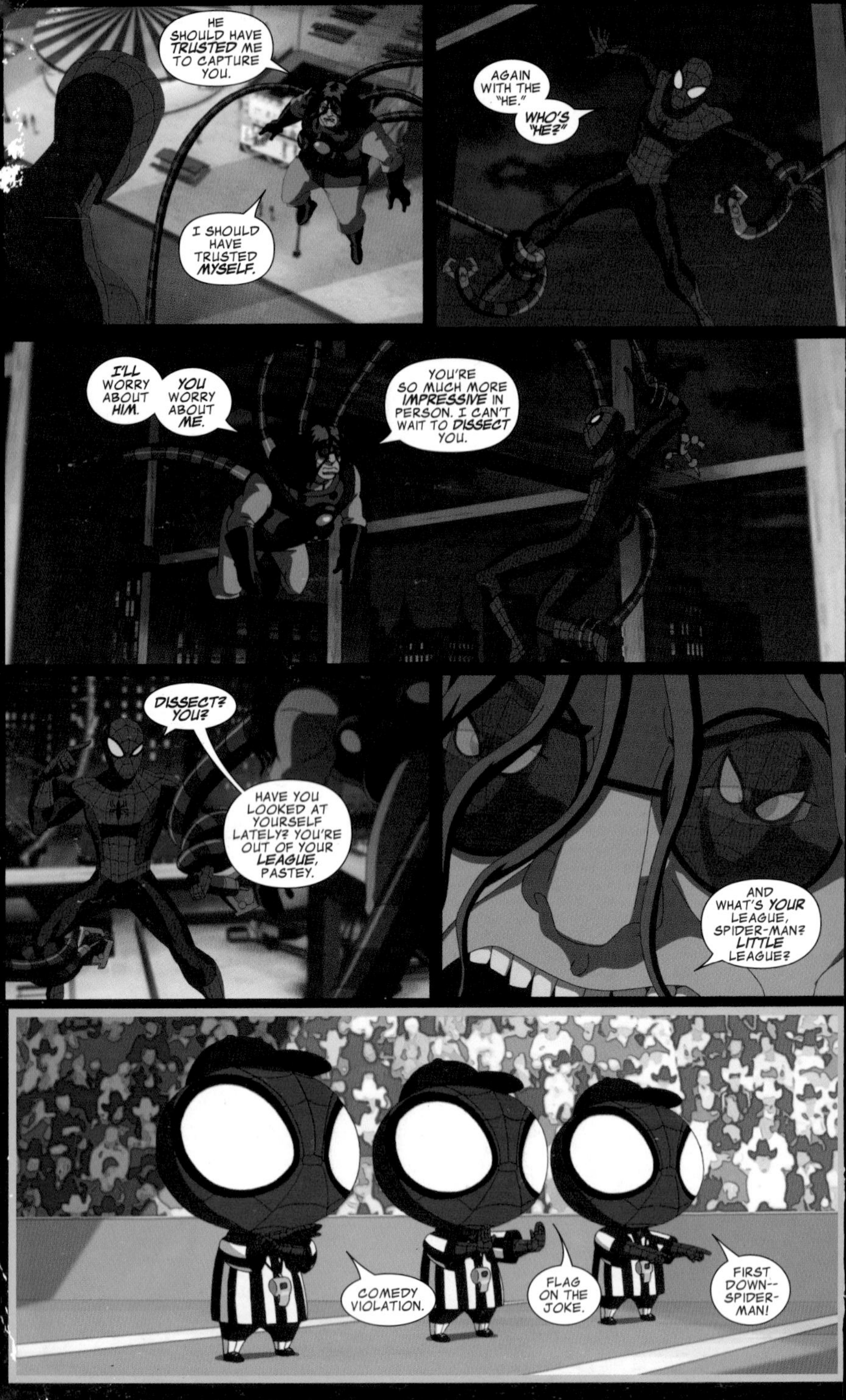
HE SHOULD HAVE TRUSTED ME TO CAPTURE YOU.
I SHOULD HAVE TRUSTED MYSELF.
AGAIN WITH THE "HE." WHO'S "HE?"
I'LL WORRY ABOUT HIM.
YOU WORRY ABOUT ME.
YOU'RE SO MUCH MORE IMPRESSIVE IN PERSON. I CAN'T WAIT TO DISSECT YOU.
DISSECT? YOU?
HAVE YOU LOOKED AT YOURSELF LATELY? YOU'RE OUT OF YOUR LEAGUE, PASTEY.
AND WHAT'S YOUR LEAGUE, SPIDER-MAN? LITTLE LEAGUE?
COMEDY VIOLATION.
FLAG ON THE JOKE.
FIRST DOWN--SPIDER-MAN!

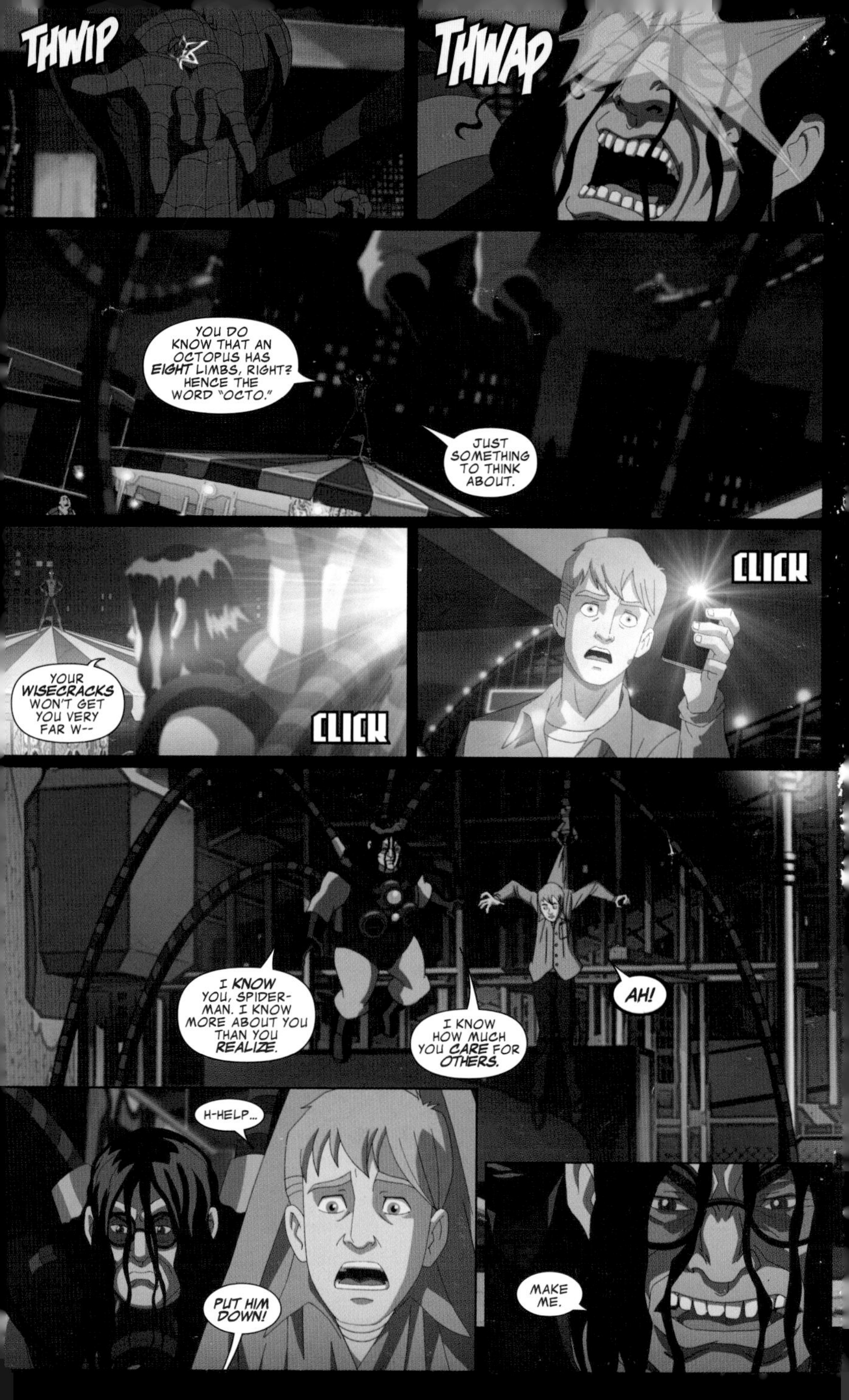
THWIP
THWAP
YOU DO KNOW THAT AN OCTOPUS HAS EIGHT LIMBS, RIGHT? HENCE THE WORD "OCTO."
JUST SOMETHING TO THINK ABOUT.
YOUR WISECRACKS WON'T GET YOU VERY FAR W--
CLICK
CLICK
I KNOW YOU, SPIDER-MAN. I KNOW MORE ABOUT YOU THAN YOU REALIZE.
I KNOW HOW MUCH YOU CARE FOR OTHERS.
AH!
H-HELP...
PUT HIM DOWN!
MAKE ME.

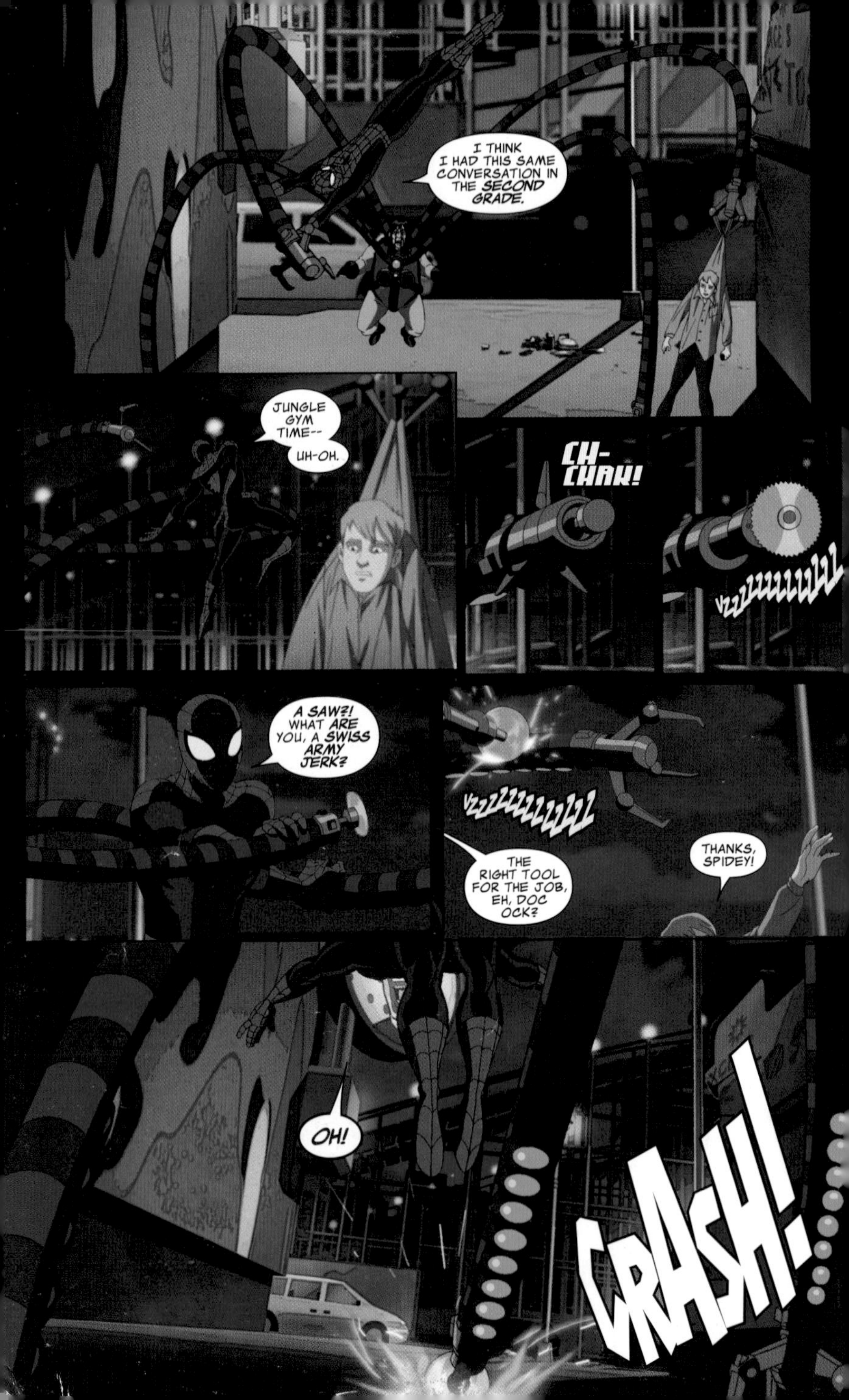
I THINK I HAD THIS SAME CONVERSATION IN THE SECOND GRADE.
JUNGLE GYM TIME--
UH-OH.
CH-CHAK!
VZZZZZZZZZZZZZZ
A SAW?! WHAT ARE YOU, A SWISS ARMY JERK?
VZZZZZZZZZZZZZZZ
THE RIGHT TOOL FOR THE JOB, EH, DOC OCK?
THANKS, SPIDEY!
OH!
CRASH!

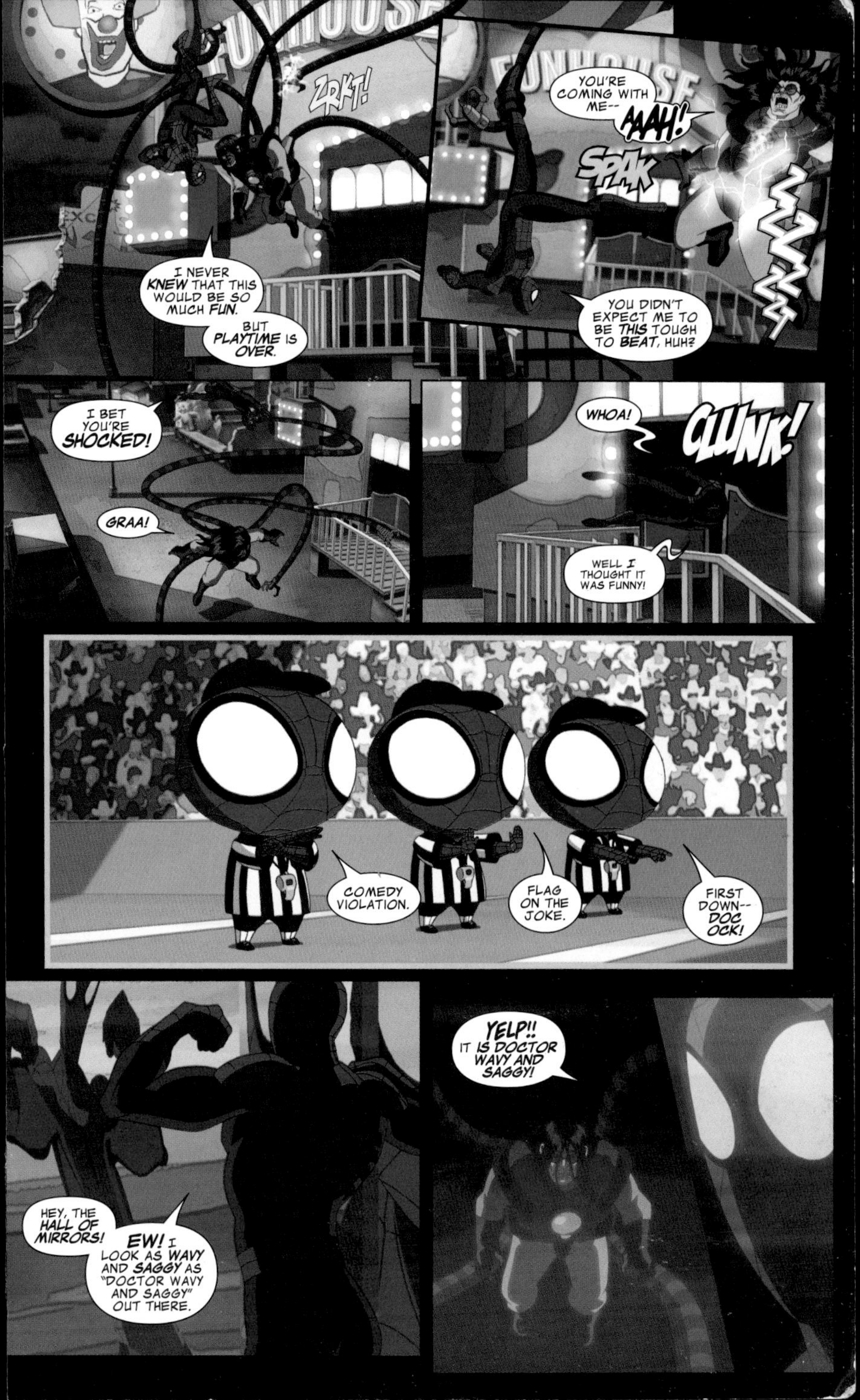
FUNHOUSE
ZRKT!
I NEVER KNEW THAT THIS WOULD BE SO MUCH FUN.
BUT PLAYTIME IS OVER.
FUNHOUSE
YOU'RE COMING WITH ME-- AAAH!
SPAK
ZZZZZT
YOU DIDN'T EXPECT ME TO BE THIS TOUGH TO BEAT, HUH?
I BET YOU'RE SHOCKED!
GRAA!
WHOA!
CLUNK!
WELL I THOUGHT IT WAS FUNNY!
COMEDY VIOLATION.
FLAG ON THE JOKE.
FIRST DOWN-- DOC OCK!
HEY, THE HALL OF MIRRORS!
EW! I LOOK AS WAVY AND SAGGY AS "DOCTOR WAVY AND SAGGY" OUT THERE.
YELP!! IT IS DOCTOR WAVY AND SAGGY!

I DIDN'T ALWAYS LOOK THIS WAY. I WAS YOUNG AND *HANDSOME* ONCE.

BEFORE... BEFORE THE *ACCIDENT*...

I'M SURE IF YOU ASK NICELY THEY MIGHT LET YOU KEEP ONE OF THESE DISTORTION MIRRORS.

YOU'RE TRYING MY *TEMPER!*

YEAH. AND I DON'T LIKE IT.

SMASH!

COMEDY VIOLATION.

FLAG ON THE JOKE.

FIRST DOWN-- DOC--

OH, COME *ON!* THAT WAS *FUNNY!*

I TRIED HIS TEMPER, AND DIDN'T LIKE IT!

GET IT?!

YOU'RE COMING WITH ME!

OVER MY DEAD BODY!

IF YOU INSIST!

OGGIE OGGIE OGGIE

ZZZRRRRAAAKKKKKK

"INCOMING CALL FROM *DOCTOR OCTAVIUS*..."

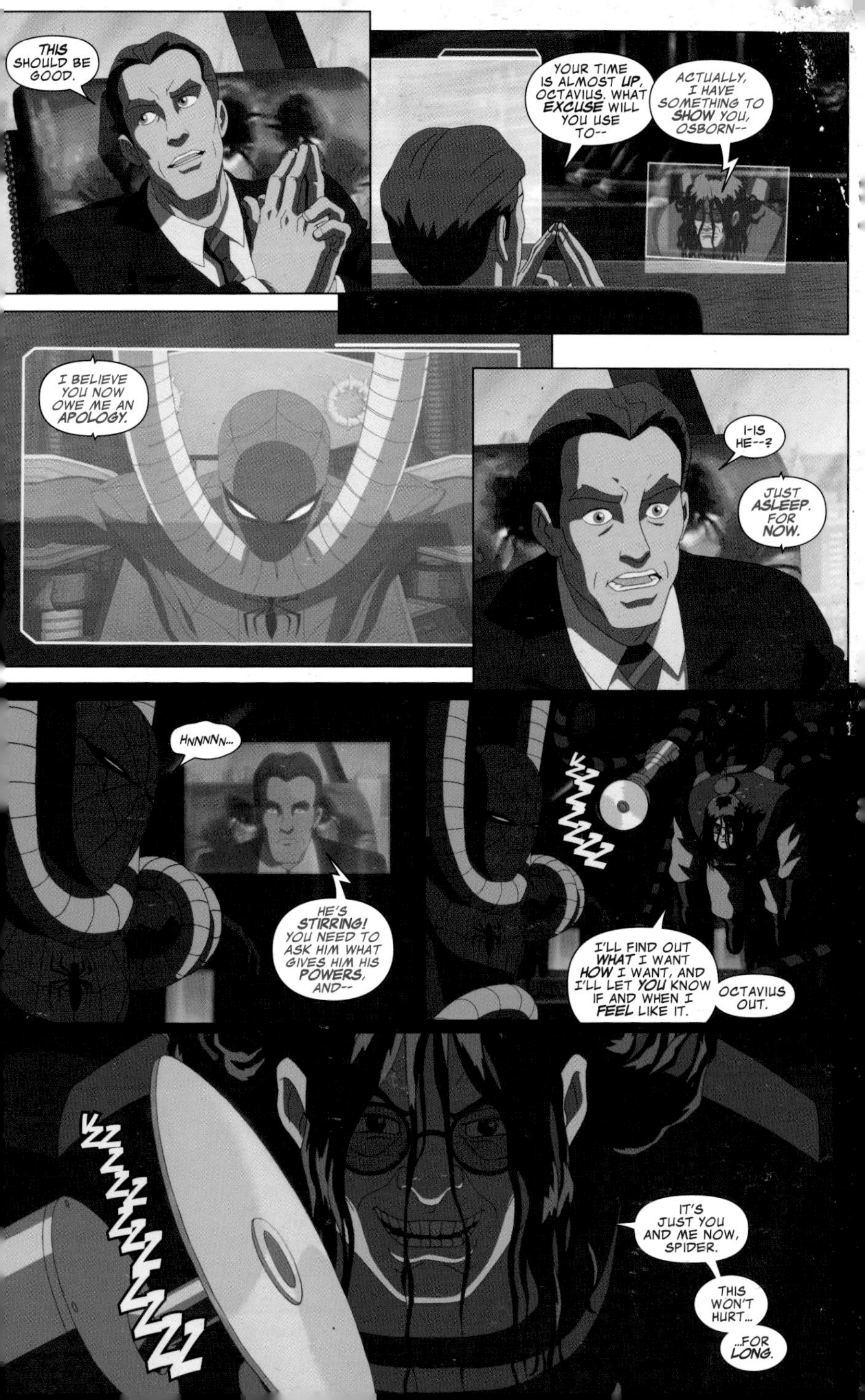
THIS SHOULD BE GOOD.
YOUR TIME IS ALMOST UP, OCTAVIUS. WHAT EXCUSE WILL YOU USE TO--
ACTUALLY, I HAVE SOMETHING TO SHOW YOU, OSBORN--
I BELIEVE YOU NOW OWE ME AN APOLOGY.
I-IS HE--?
JUST ASLEEP. FOR NOW.
HNNNNN...
HE'S STIRRING! YOU NEED TO ASK HIM WHAT GIVES HIM HIS POWERS, AND--
VZZZZZ
I'LL FIND OUT WHAT I WANT HOW I WANT, AND I'LL LET YOU KNOW IF AND WHEN I FEEL LIKE IT.
OCTAVIUS OUT.
VZZZZZZZZ
IT'S JUST YOU AND ME NOW, SPIDER.
THIS WON'T HURT...
...FOR LONG.

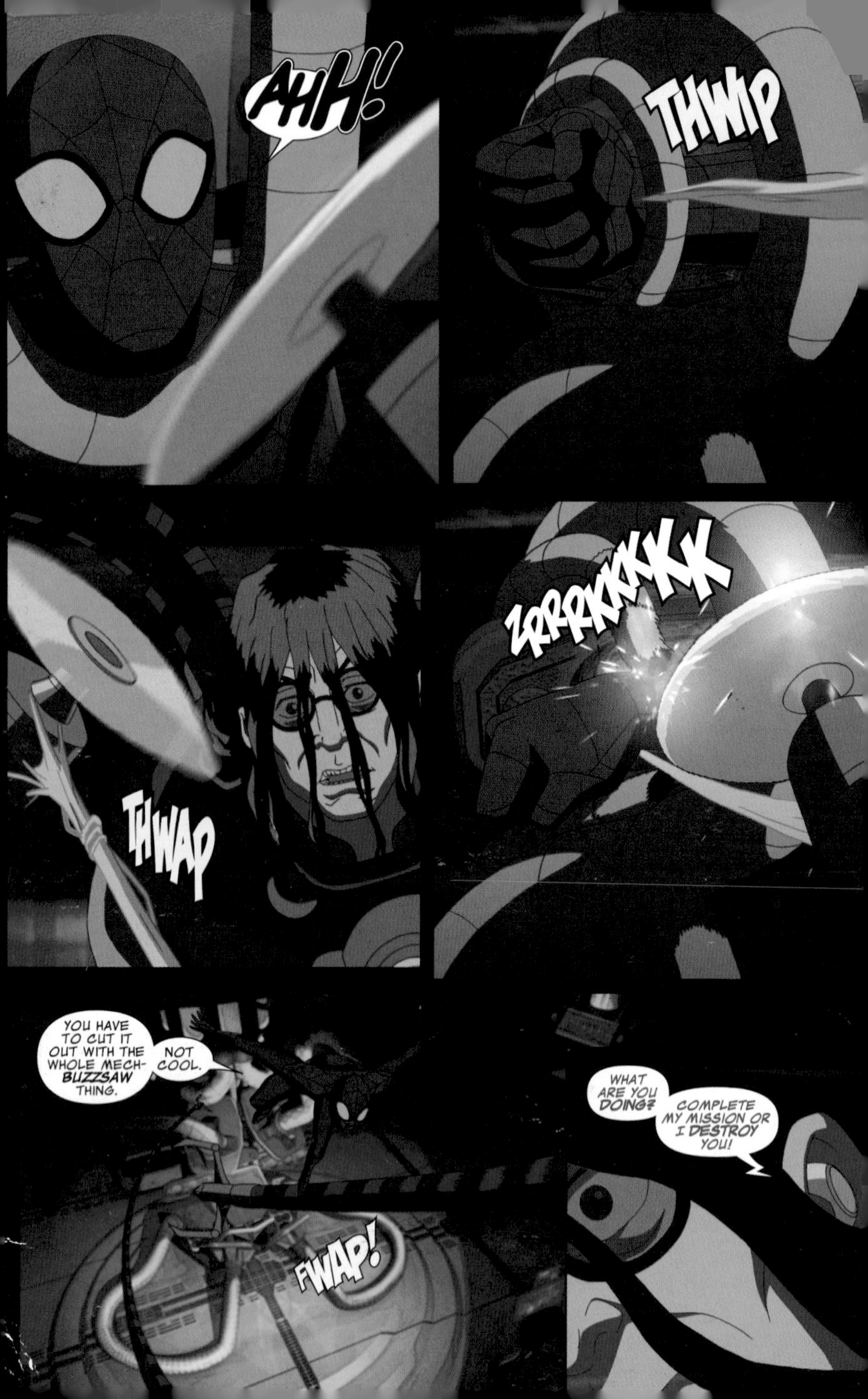
AHH!
THWIP
THWAP
ZRRRKKKKK
YOU HAVE TO CUT IT OUT WITH THE WHOLE MECH-BUZZSAW THING.
NOT COOL.
FWAP!
WHAT ARE YOU DOING?
COMPLETE MY MISSION OR I DESTROY YOU!

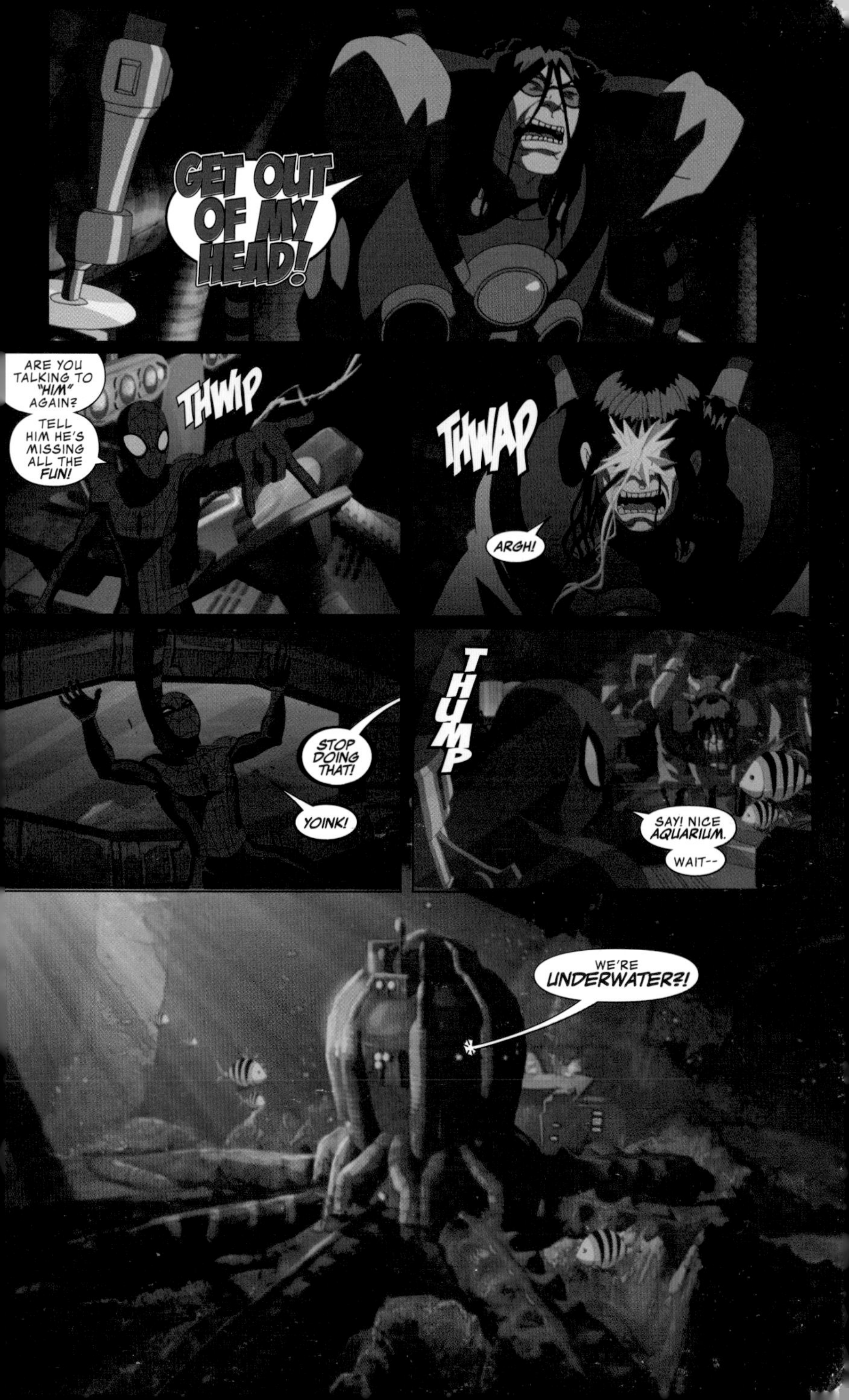
GET OUT OF MY HEAD!
ARE YOU TALKING TO "HIM" AGAIN?
TELL HIM HE'S MISSING ALL THE FUN!
THWIP
THWAP
ARGH!
STOP DOING THAT!
YOINK!
THUMP
SAY! NICE AQUARIUM.
WAIT--
WE'RE UNDERWATER?!

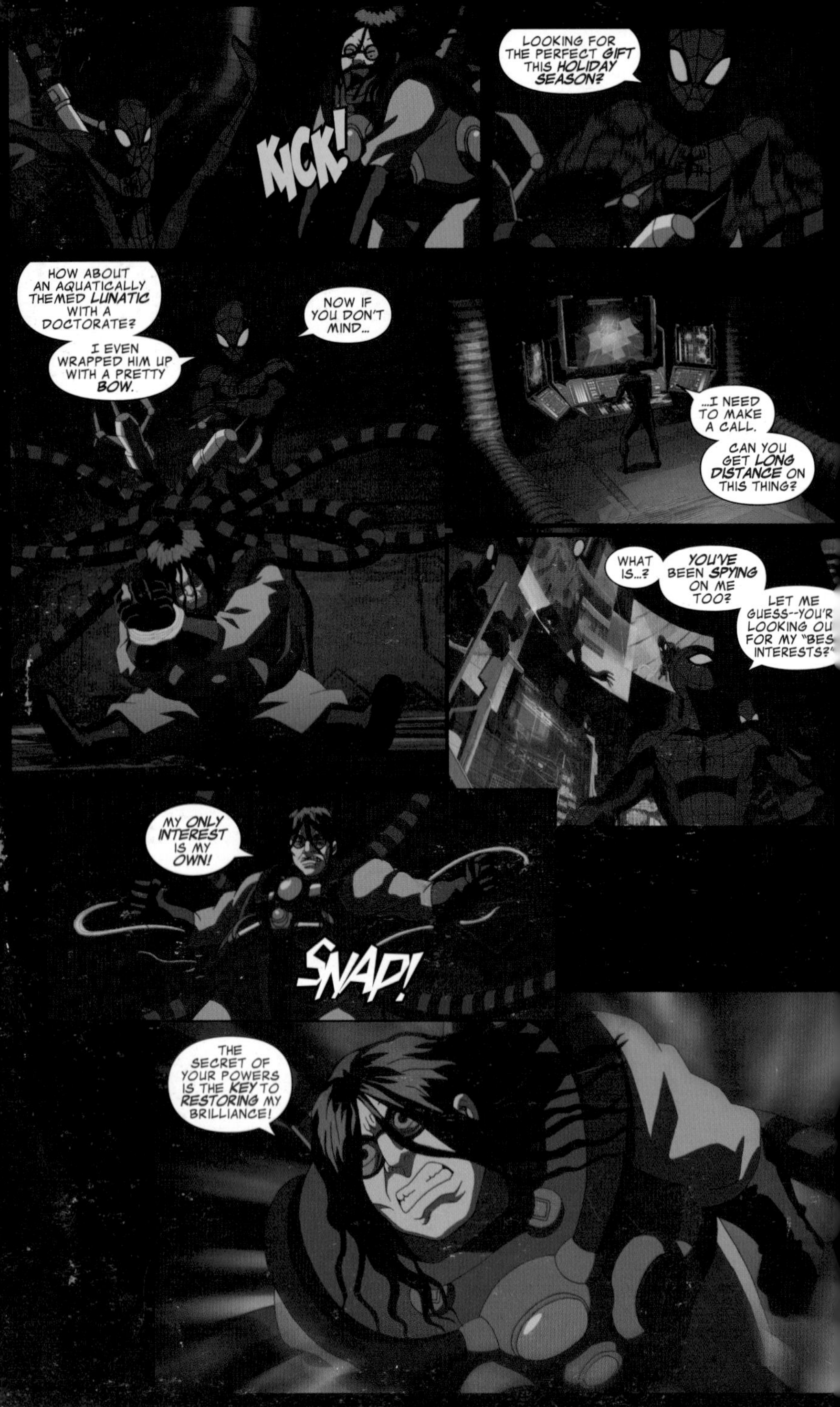
KICK!
LOOKING FOR THE PERFECT GIFT THIS HOLIDAY SEASON?
HOW ABOUT AN AQUATICALLY THEMED LUNATIC WITH A DOCTORATE?
I EVEN WRAPPED HIM UP WITH A PRETTY BOW.
NOW IF YOU DON'T MIND...
...I NEED TO MAKE A CALL.
CAN YOU GET LONG DISTANCE ON THIS THING?
WHAT IS...?
YOU'VE BEEN SPYING ON ME TOO?
LET ME GUESS--YOU'R LOOKING OU FOR MY "BES INTERESTS?"
MY ONLY INTEREST IS MY OWN!
SNAP!
THE SECRET OF YOUR POWERS IS THE KEY TO RESTORING MY BRILLIANCE!

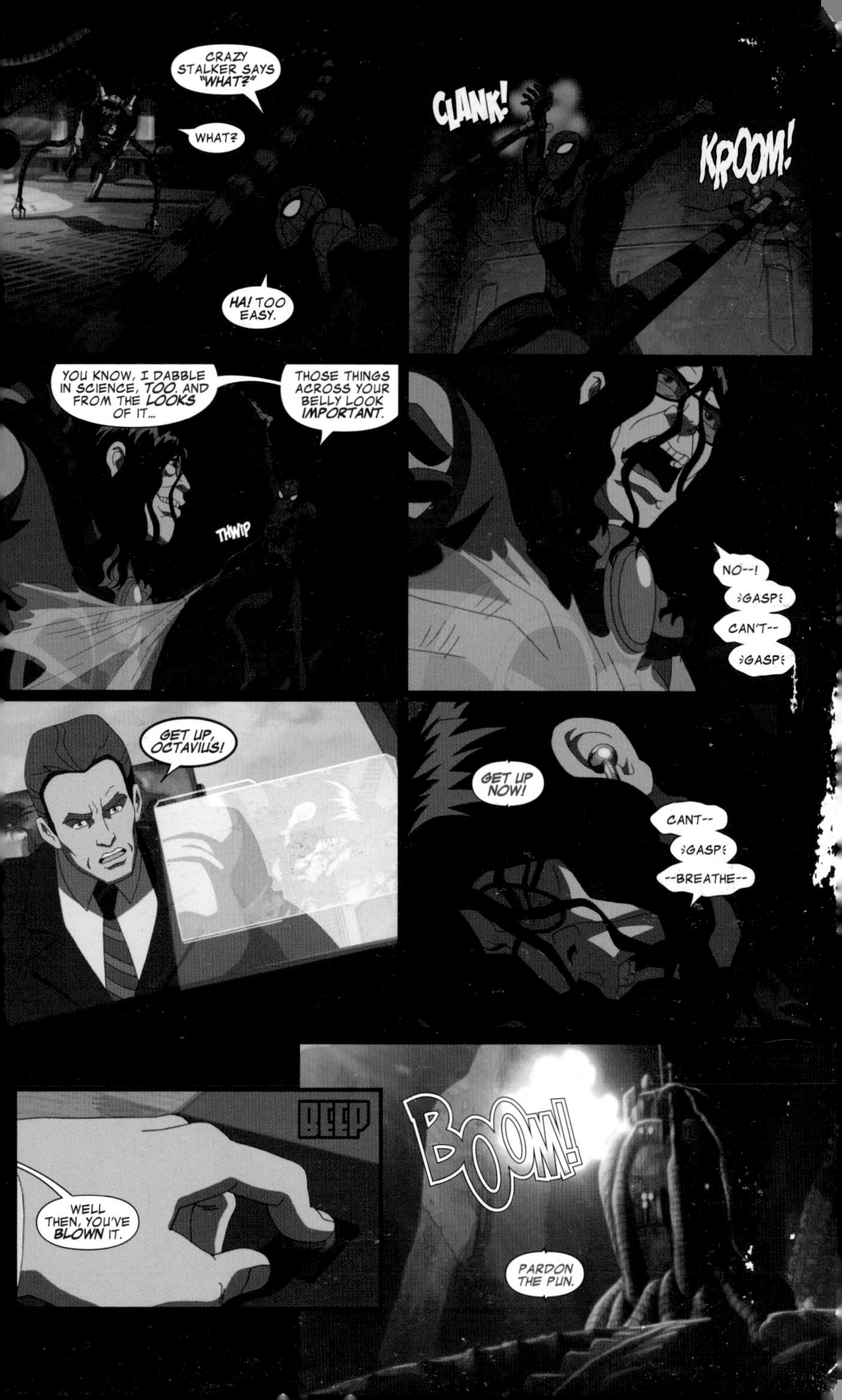
CRAZY STALKER SAYS "WHAT?"
WHAT?
HA! TOO EASY.
CLANK!
KROOM!
YOU KNOW, I DABBLE IN SCIENCE, TOO. AND FROM THE LOOKS OF IT...
THOSE THINGS ACROSS YOUR BELLY LOOK IMPORTANT.
THWIP
NO--!
GASP
CAN'T--
GASP
GET UP, OCTAVIUS!
GET UP NOW!
CANT--
GASP
--BREATHE--
BEEP
WELL THEN, YOU'VE BLOWN IT.
BOOM!
PARDON THE PUN.

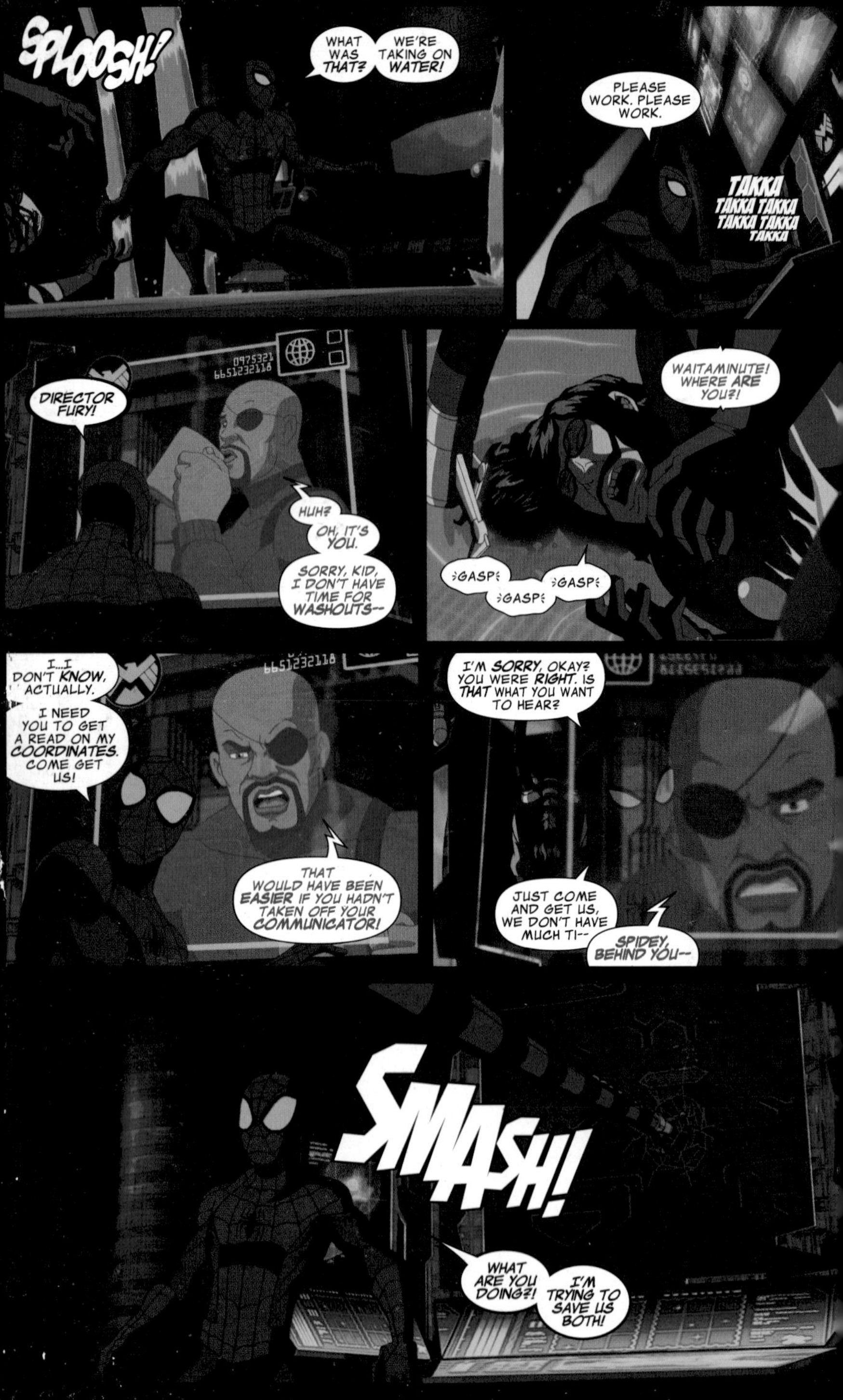
SPLOOSH!
WHAT WAS THAT?
WE'RE TAKING ON WATER!
PLEASE WORK. PLEASE WORK.
TAKKA TAKKA TAKKA TAKKA TAKKA TAKKA
DIRECTOR FURY!
HUH?
OH, IT'S YOU.
SORRY, KID, I DON'T HAVE TIME FOR WASHOUTS--
WAITAMINUTE! WHERE ARE YOU?!
GASP GASP GASP
I...I DON'T KNOW, ACTUALLY.
I NEED YOU TO GET A READ ON MY COORDINATES. COME GET US!
THAT WOULD HAVE BEEN EASIER IF YOU HADN'T TAKEN OFF YOUR COMMUNICATOR!
I'M SORRY, OKAY? YOU WERE RIGHT. IS THAT WHAT YOU WANT TO HEAR?
JUST COME AND GET US, WE DON'T HAVE MUCH TI--
SPIDEY, BEHIND YOU--
SMASH!
WHAT ARE YOU DOING?!
I'M TRYING TO SAVE US BOTH!

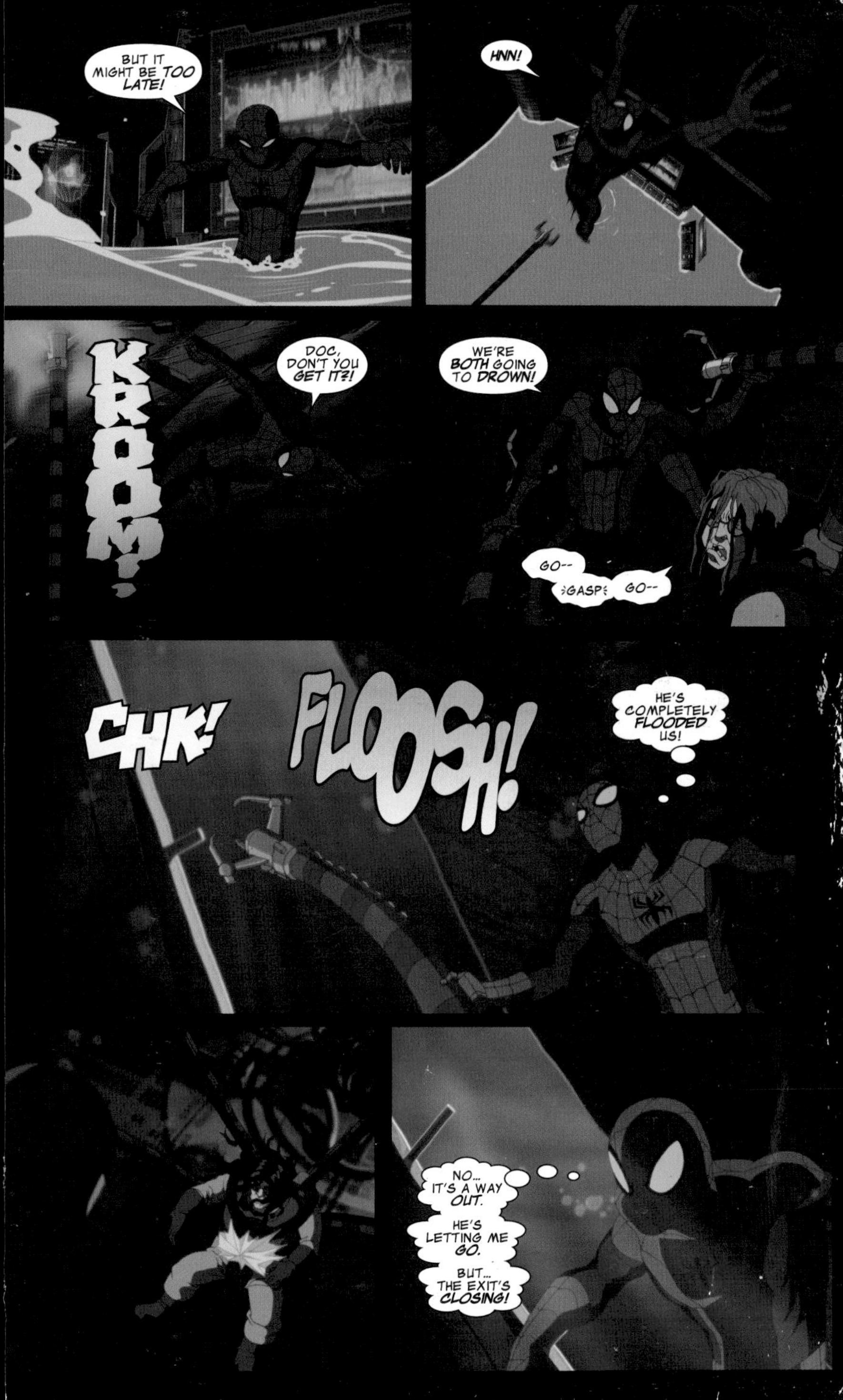
BUT IT MIGHT BE TOO LATE!
HNN!
KROOM!
DOC, DON'T YOU GET IT?!
WE'RE BOTH GOING TO DROWN!
GO--
GASP GO--
CHK!
FLOOSH!
HE'S COMPLETELY FLOODED US!
NO... IT'S A WAY OUT.
HE'S LETTING ME GO.
BUT... THE EXIT'S CLOSING!

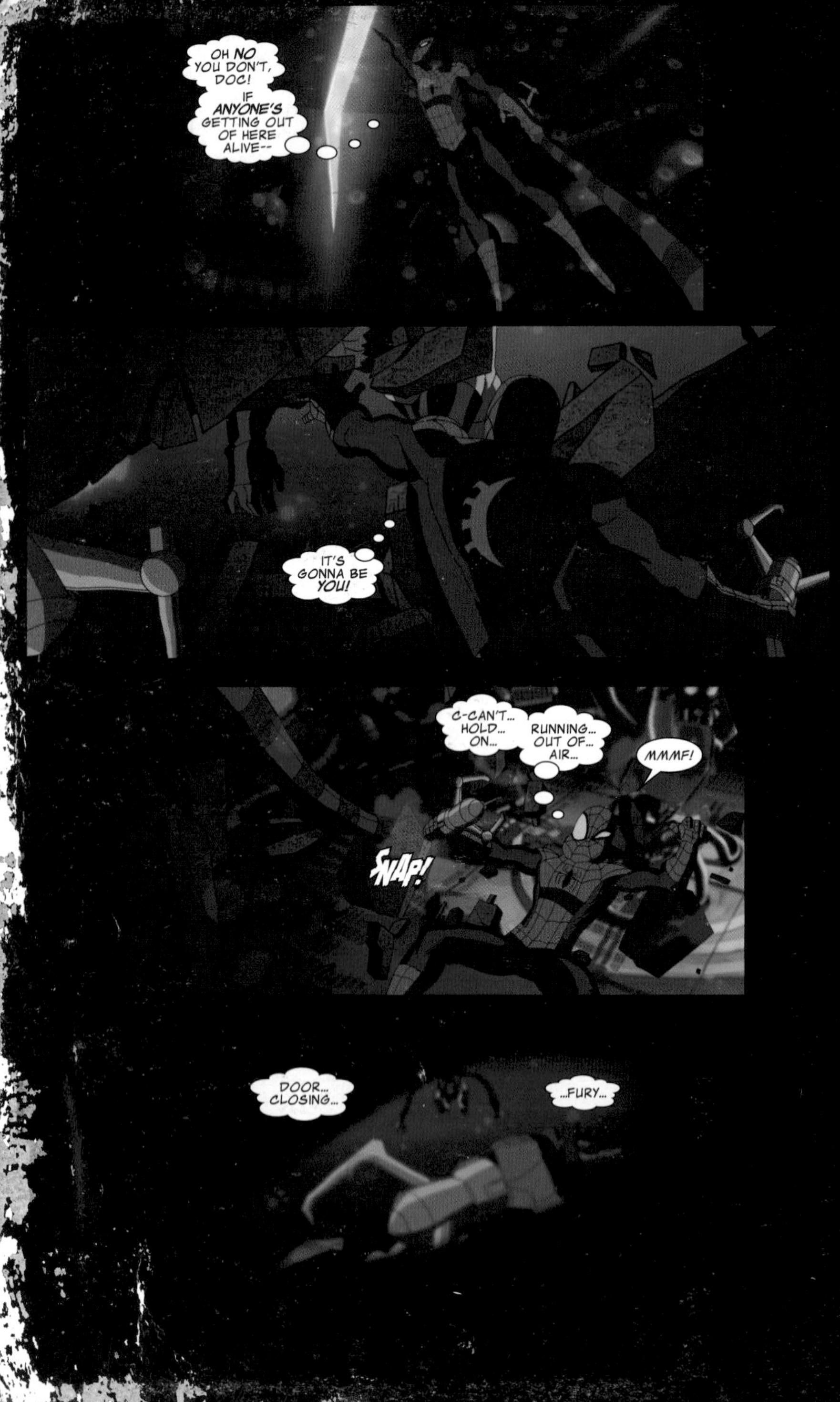
OH NO YOU DON'T, DOC!
IF ANYONE'S GETTING OUT OF HERE ALIVE--
IT'S GONNA BE YOU!
C-CAN'T... HOLD... ON...
RUNNING... OUT OF... AIR...
MMMF!
SNAP!
DOOR... CLOSING...
...FURY...

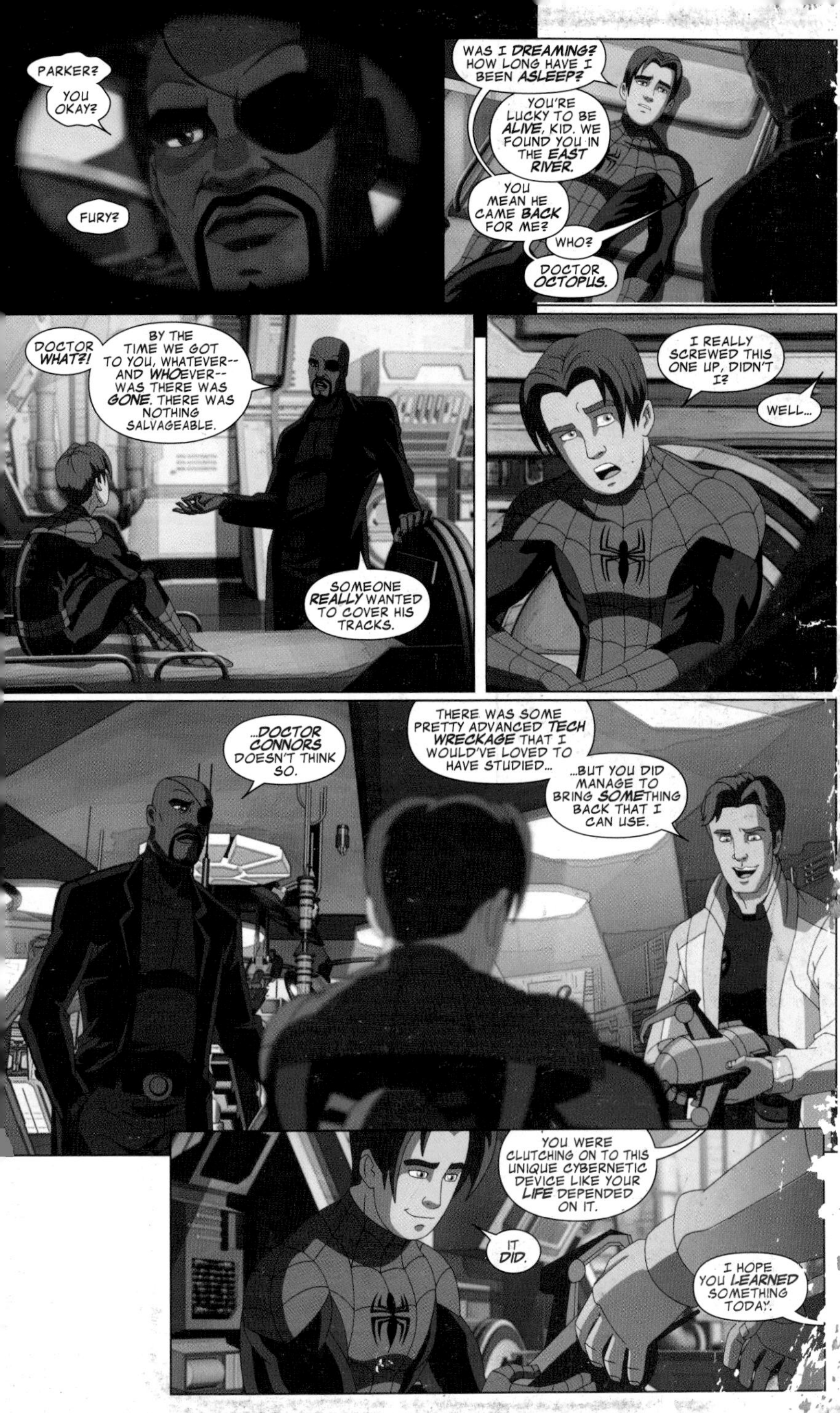
PARKER?
YOU OKAY?
FURY?
WAS I DREAMING? HOW LONG HAVE I BEEN ASLEEP?
YOU'RE LUCKY TO BE ALIVE, KID. WE FOUND YOU IN THE EAST RIVER.
YOU MEAN HE CAME BACK FOR ME?
WHO?
DOCTOR OCTOPUS.
DOCTOR WHAT?!
BY THE TIME WE GOT TO YOU, WHATEVER--AND WHOEVER--WAS THERE WAS GONE. THERE WAS NOTHING SALVAGEABLE.
SOMEONE REALLY WANTED TO COVER HIS TRACKS.
I REALLY SCREWED THIS ONE UP, DIDN'T I?
WELL...
...DOCTOR CONNORS DOESN'T THINK SO.
THERE WAS SOME PRETTY ADVANCED TECH WRECKAGE THAT I WOULD'VE LOVED TO HAVE STUDIED...
...BUT YOU DID MANAGE TO BRING SOMETHING BACK THAT I CAN USE.
YOU WERE CLUTCHING ON TO THIS UNIQUE CYBERNETIC DEVICE LIKE YOUR LIFE DEPENDED ON IT.
IT DID.
I HOPE YOU LEARNED SOMETHING TODAY.

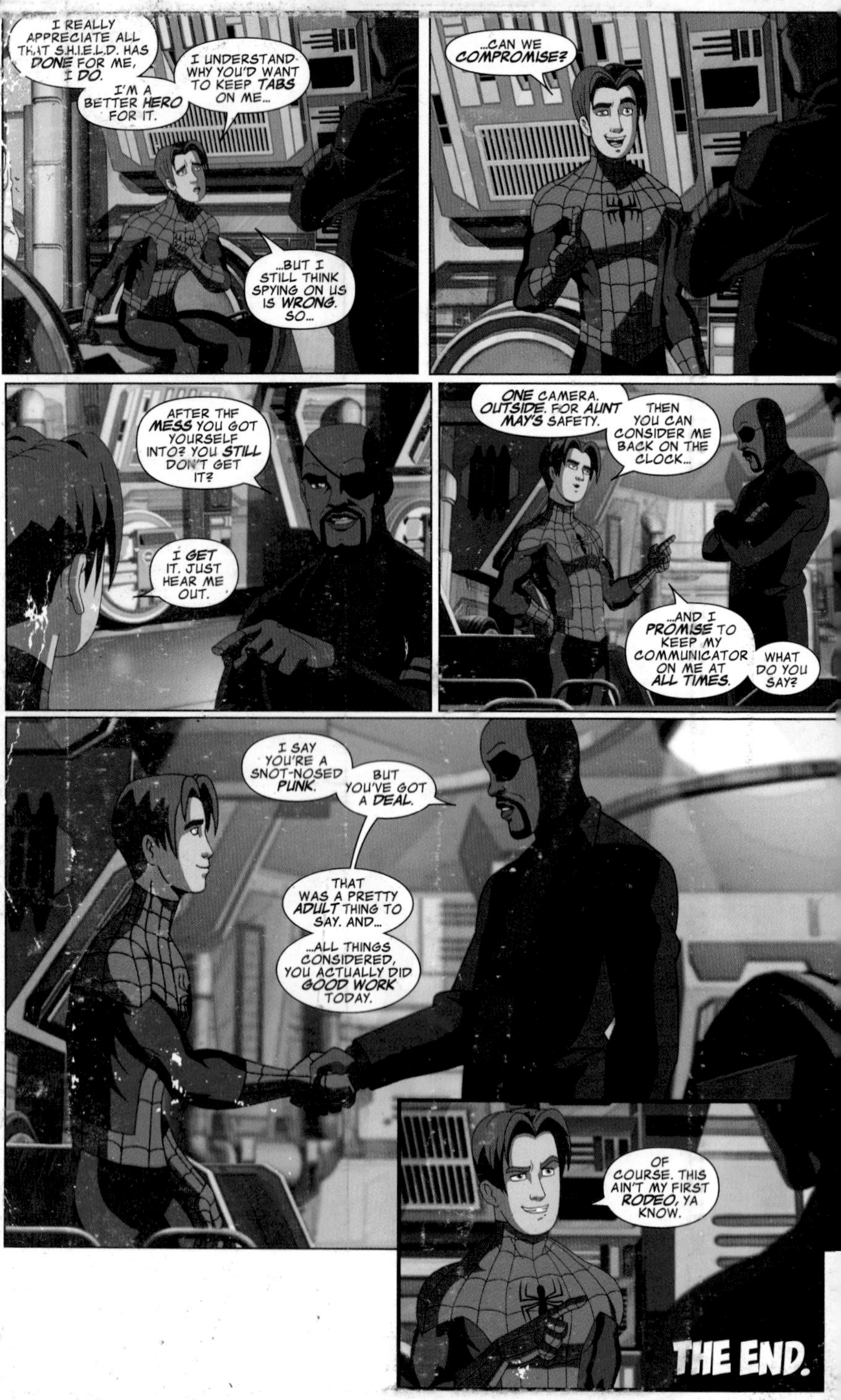

I REALLY APPRECIATE ALL THAT S.H.I.E.L.D. HAS DONE FOR ME, I DO.
I'M A BETTER HERO FOR IT.
I UNDERSTAND WHY YOU'D WANT TO KEEP TABS ON ME...
...BUT I STILL THINK SPYING ON US IS WRONG. SO...
...CAN WE COMPROMISE?
AFTER THE MESS YOU GOT YOURSELF INTO? YOU STILL DON'T GET IT?
I GET IT. JUST HEAR ME OUT.
ONE CAMERA. OUTSIDE. FOR AUNT MAY'S SAFETY.
THEN YOU CAN CONSIDER ME BACK ON THE CLOCK...
...AND I PROMISE TO KEEP MY COMMUNICATOR ON ME AT ALL TIMES.
WHAT DO YOU SAY?
I SAY YOU'RE A SNOT-NOSED PUNK.
BUT YOU'VE GOT A DEAL.
THAT WAS A PRETTY ADULT THING TO SAY. AND...
...ALL THINGS CONSIDERED, YOU ACTUALLY DID GOOD WORK TODAY.
OF COURSE. THIS AIN'T MY FIRST RODEO, YA KNOW.
THE END.